Religion **to** Relationship
Convenience **to** Consistency

THE JOURNEY TO FULFILLING PURPOSE

DAEJAH MERRILL

Paperback: 978-1-7351153-0-6
Ebook: 978-1-7351153-2-0

Cover art by Anthony Parker Jr.
Layout by HMDgfx.com

To my best friend, Lawrion. Thank you for shining your light and loving me with the love of God. Without you I truly don't know where I would be. Thank you for seeing the best in me when I couldn't.

Contents

Part One:

PAIN INTO PURPOSE

Part Two:

RELIGION TO RELATIONSHIP

Part Three:

CONVENIENCE TO CONSISTENCY

Christianity Is Not Just a Religion, It's a Lifestyle

Christianity is not something that is to be practiced only on Sunday. It is not something that is to be picked up and put down for convenience. Christianity is not supposed to be a religion where you have to act or dress the part. Being a Christian does not mean you have it all together, but you are working to become a better version of yourself each day. Christianity should not just be seen as a religion, a routine or system of faith and worship, but Christianity should be a personal relationship with God that will ultimately cause a life transformation.

God's will for your life is to become a new creature by striving to be more like him and live beyond your comfort level by choosing to develop a new level of thinking and walking in purpose. Some Christians are living below the privileges of the life that God has promised them. Some Christians are still carrying around hurt, bitterness, unforgiveness, hate, and selfishness on the inside, but they look the part on the outside. So many people are trying to praise their way through in church, but still go home dealing with the weight of anxiety and depression with no hope that God can heal them. I know this because I used to be one of them that suffered in silence.

God works from the inside out, but some never allow God to heal their wounds because they never speak to God about it. Throughout their lives, they carry pain that can be passed on to those they are connected to unintentionally, and it becomes a cycle that seems never to be broken. Get ready because the cycle can be broken with you. Growing up as a church kid, I felt as if I had to live a double life. I was using the church as a place to make me feel happy, but the feeling was always temporary. It wasn't the feeling of relief and freedom that I felt daily. Throughout my week, I dealt with reality: with my real issues, real pain, and my real shortcomings.

My reality is somewhere I never invited God to be. I had believed the misconception and limited God's presence to a building. Church made me "feel" good, but my reality was nothing like it. At some point, I got tired of acting, I reached a breaking point, and I realized that I had to be vulnerable and transparent about the real me. God cannot do anything with the person you try to be; he wants to work on the real you. This is a life that he never intended for you to live alone. When you acknowledge God, he will direct your paths. His guidance is something you can trust. The Bible says he will never put more on you than you can bear. The weight and burden that you are still carrying; God wants you to know that you were never meant to carry that alone. Some battles are not yours to fight, so give it to the Lord.

He died so that you could be you and ultimately live your life in and for him. The freedom or "good feeling" that was once temporary became everlasting. I had truly experienced God for myself. Once I opened up my reality to God, I was able to see that this walk with God is supposed to become a lifestyle. When you allow God full access to all of you, you can release all your pain, worry, doubt, and fear to him so that you can live the abundant life that he has promised.

John 10:10(NKJV) – The thief does not come except to steal, and to kill, and to destroy. I have come that they may have life and that they may have it more abundantly.
2 Corinthians 5:15(NLT) – He died for everyone so that those who receive his new life will no longer live for themselves. Instead, they will live for Christ, who died and was raised for them.

Christ died for everyone; he rose and conquered death, hell, and the grave, and rules with all power in his hands. There is life after any situation that seems dead. The same power that raised Jesus from the dead is the same power that lives in you. So, if you have not already, you have the opportunity to give your life to Christ.

Romans 10:9-10(GNT) - If you confess that Jesus is Lord and believe that God raised him from death, you will be saved. For it is by our faith that we are put right with God; it is by our confession that we are saved.

If you are already saved, I challenge you to live a life beyond the infancy stage of salvation, and give God total access, so that you may fulfill the purpose of your life. Some Christians choose to have faith only in certain situations and attach God's name to things they did not believe could be produced, until it happened. Some try to attach his name to things he was not in from the beginning, like un-ordained relationships, and self-centered businesses, or career paths.

Hebrews 11:1(KJV) - Now faith is the substance of things hoped for, the evidence of things not seen.

Having faith in God allows you to change your perspective on many life situations. Faith gives you the ability to speak life over a situation that looks dead. Having faith allows you to believe anything is possible even if you physically can't see it yet. Christianity is supposed to be an ongoing walk where your trust remains in God in every situation. God can give you peace that will surpass all understanding, joy that will be your strength amid a storm, and hope for a better future. You will begin to stand out amongst people because your response to a crisis is different. Your response to a problem or an unexpected shift is different. Committing your life to Christ means that you choose God's way over your way and his mindset over your own. When you let God into your heart, you allow him to produce things in your life that you could never do without him, both naturally and spiritually.

> *Psalms 1:3(AMP) - And he will be like a tree firmly planted [and fed] by streams of water, Which yields its fruit in its season; Its leaf does not wither; And in whatever he does, he prospers [and comes to maturity].*

Only planted trees can bear fruit. Planted means being deeply rooted in God's design for your life. Once the seed (you) is planted, it grows roots, the roots take hold of your faith, and a small plant will emerge and break through the soil. Your emersion through the soil represents you breaking through anything that used to hold you bound. The soil which provides nutrients for the seed represents the healthy environment this plant needs to survive. You will need a strong godly community and a church home to worship and be led. This plant needs three things to help it grow: consistent light (God), daily food (word of God), and water (prayer and fasting, praise, and worship). The light gives the plant energy to undergo photosynthesis, the process of converting light into food.

When you are in the light, God produces purpose through you. Darkness is a place where there is no purpose. You were in the dark long enough, but the moment you come into the light and identify who you are in Christ, purpose can be produced. As you grow, you need to feed yourself daily with God's word, and you must water or sustain yourself with prayer, fasting, praise, and worship. The water can symbolize tears at vulnerable moments in prayer and worship. The Bible says, they that sow in tears shall reap in joy (Psalms 126:5). You must devote yourself in prayer, and praise shall continually be in your mouth, despite any circumstance.

Praise expresses happiness or relief that something did or did not happen. Worship is deeper than praise; worship exposes you because it expresses an extreme form of love for God, and God wants us to worship him in spirit and in truth. As the plant begins to grow, the roots continue to grow to allow you to go deeper in God and in your faith. I cannot describe what happens on the inside of the seed as it comes to life because everyone's journey is different; you should not follow or compare your journey with other people.

Every person's journey is unique, and you can only win and receive what God has for you in your lane. Embracing this change and walking in freedom from things that used to keep you bound will not be easy, but it is not impossible. Some choose just to hide their pain and try to keep it all together in their own strength. Behavior manipulation is easier than embracing transformation and freedom from bondage, freedom sometimes hurts, but manipulation is just controlling someone or something to a certain point for your own advantage.

Behavior manipulation is you saying no to yourself and making rules; you must abide by. However, transformation takes God, and you being obedient to him. For transformation to take place, you initially have to admit that you have imperfections, struggles and that you cannot do life alone. Transformation and growth take time and commitment; you have to remain committed to becoming a better you. Christianity is supposed to be something that is lived out each day. In Christ, you find your identity and purpose, and you learn to appreciate why God has even allowed you to survive the things you have been through because he has plans for you.

Jeremiah 29:11(NLT) - For I know the plans I have for you, says the Lord. They are plans for good and not for disaster, to give you a future and a hope.

When you become a believer in Christ, you have hope for a better future, with Christ you can believe that your past will not define your future, but that the pain you have endured can birth purpose. When you try God, he will come through, and when you set your mind on him and things above, he will never fail you. Christianity is supposed to be a lifestyle that puts Christ's words, methods, and instructions into practice. Being a Christian is not something that is done for show or performance, but when Christ has genuinely saved you from yourself: every adversity that tried to destroy you, he worked out for your good. Thus, your praise becomes real and genuine.

Being a child of God also empowers you. Becoming his child allows you to understand that nothing you have done or been through can separate you from the love of God.

> *Psalms 139:14(TPT) - I thank you, God, for making me so mysteriously complex! Everything you do is marvelously breathtaking. It simply amazes me to think about it! How thoroughly you know me, Lord!*
> *Philippians 4:13(NKJV) - I can do all things through Christ, who strengthens me.*
> *Romans 8:38-39(NKJV) - For I am persuaded that neither death nor life, nor angels nor principalities nor powers, nor things present nor things to come, nor height nor depth, nor any other created thing, shall be able to separate us from the love of God which is in Christ Jesus our Lord.*

Christianity is not just something you are, but it's something you have to be. God wants you to be a representation of Christ and be a living sacrifice. God allows you to be and not act. Christianity should not be an act or just a religion; it's a lifestyle! A lifestyle is a way in which a person or group lives.

> *Matthew 11:28-30(KJV) - Come unto me, all ye that labor and are heavily laden, and I will give you rest. Take my yoke upon you and learn of me; for I am meek and lowly in heart: and ye shall find rest unto your souls. For my yoke is easy, and my burden is light.*

Make Christianity a lifestyle because, with God, you won't have to try so hard to have it all together alone. It's a fixed fight; you already have the victory!

Part One:

PAIN INTO PURPOSE

Chapter One

MY TESTIMONY

At the age of nine, I was molested by a family member, and from that very moment, my innocence was taken away from me, I was taken advantage of, and I was exposed to sexual things at a young age. From that point in my life, love, and the power and sacredness of sex were perverted. My mind was corrupted, and from that point, I struggled silently for a couple of years without saying anything to anyone in fear of breaking my family apart, in fear of being judged, and in fear of no one believing me. My silence birthed insecurities, depression, and lack of self-worth, and it gave room for the enemy to come in and begin to torment my mind to the point where I didn't even see a point in living. I was physically alive, but I was spiritually, mentally, and emotionally drained.

I finally spoke up about it after it occurred again at age eleven. I spoke up because I feared that my predator could have been hurting others like my little sisters and cousins. I wanted to save them from experiencing something that should've destroyed me, but what the enemy meant for evil, God turned it around for my good. I had told my parents, my family, and members of my home church even knew. I remember going to family court; I remember having to repeat my story over many times. I also remember how I felt when he was not sentenced to jail because it was just a first-time offense. I remember having to cross paths with him going to and from school or work: I remember fearing to see him at family gatherings and even church. I remember trying to avoid him at any chance I got. I remember feeling like "He did the crime, but I was doing time."

I felt like there was no point in speaking up, I felt defeated, I felt weak and alone, and no one could understand the pain that I felt. I also remember trying to praise my way through it every time I stepped foot into my church and acted as if I was okay. I remember the great act I put on, I smiled on the outside, but internally I was suffering. Even though I spoke up about it, I never truly healed from the trauma I had faced.

I went to church because it was a routine that was instilled in me from a very young age. I followed the rules and respected the doctrine that was taught and enforced. I remember believing that if I followed the rules that God would love me more. Deep down inside, I did not believe that God really loved me because I did not believe he could allow me to go through such pain.

I went for therapy, and I believe that it helped to a certain extent. I then experienced church hurt because the situation was swept under the rug as if it had no effect on me and my future. I was church hurt because I was judged when I started falling short of the glory of God. I was judged, but never offered a prayer of deliverance or restoration. I was just looked at as a problem child, and I can see why because when I look back, I can say I was lost. I was a lost young girl attempting to find myself. I grew into a young teenager with a lot of pain and anger built up inside that I never released. I became comfortable and accustomed to pain and hurt. It became something that I expected; it was something that I thought I deserved.

As I grew older, I started acting out sexually, looking for love in all the wrong places. Seeking attention from men because I was looking for something to fill this void, I was looking for fulfillment. I also begin to make myself busy being involved in things I enjoyed, but it also was a way to distract myself from dealing with the real issue. I started working and making my own money. I started being involved in things at school because I didn't want to be home; I felt misunderstood. I suffered in silence, I didn't love myself or who I was becoming, and it was very evident.

I kept a smile on my face, and in the church, I sang songs in the choir, praise danced, and helped out where I could. I later realized that God gave me the gift of dance. Dance was the first time I was able to get vulnerable, honest, and intimate with God. Dance was a way I could express myself without having to say anything.

Dance was a way for me to release stress, hurt, fear, and anxiety. There was a time that dance even became my god; it was something I used to put before God until I surrendered the gift to him so that he could use it for his glory. I faced depression, I had suicidal thoughts, I felt like everything terrible kept happening to me, and I begin to question God and ask him questions like. "Why me? Will this pain ever end?"

The devil used to torment me with thoughts like "It was your fault, you deserved it, you asked for it, God hates you." The truth was I became a version of myself that I hated, I disappointed myself. But this was all covered up by my achievements in school and extra-curricular activities. That version of me was tolerated, and some just ignored or could not see how wounded I was.

Because I was hurt, I acted in hurt, I acted in insecurity, and I spoke from a place of defeat. I didn't love me, so I just fought for others to love me. As the years went on, I begin to run farther and farther away from God. He seemed so far away; little did I know that God was and still is the only one who can satisfy my needs. God looked beyond my faults and saw my needs, but I first had to be real and honest and want to be healed.

I was introduced to alcohol around age 18, and that's when I started using that to fill the void, I could've lost my life because I used to get drunk and even blacked out three times. I came home one time so drunk, and after that, I was so embarrassed because my younger sisters saw that, and I felt like a disappointment to my parents. Through it all, I was hurting, I was broken, and I was desperate, yet silently crying for help. I kept dancing, and it was evident that I was different because when I danced, I told a story. It was the one place where I could be and express myself. At this age, I also met my biological father for the first time, and at this moment, I begin to deal with my daddy issues that once used to lie dormant. I chose to go to my heavenly father to heal from the pain caused by his absence. I was blessed to have a stepfather who stepped in his place, and he is someone I call Dad to this day. But either your father was present or absent in your life, we all deal with daddy issues. Our heavenly father wants us to accept his love.

Psalms 68:5(NIV) – A father to the fatherless, a defender of widows, is God in his holy dwelling.

After embracing the opportunity to meet my biological father, there were still times where he let me down, and because of poor choices, he has fallen victim to a cycle of being in and out of jail, which still hurts my heart to this day. I developed trust issues, and I once had a mindset that I was never good enough for a man's love because my own biological father failed me in many ways. But after accepting God's love and allowing him to heal me and forgive, I have been able to turn my pain and tears into praise and prayer and to trust that the same transformation that has occurred in my life, God has given my father the same grace, what he has done for me he is able to do for him.

I've had many doubts, but sometimes when we pray and ask God for something, and the results do not come when we want them, we tend to give up and stop praying. Over the years, I have learned that persistent prayers develop consistent faith, and patience develops strength and endurance. I have peace about this situation because I know that if I stay focused on what God wants to do in my life, I pray and believe that whatever he is going to do in my father's life is already done.

Psalms 138:8(NLT) - The Lord will work out his plans for my life—for your faithful love, O Lord, endures forever. Don't abandon me, for you made me.
Psalms 27:13(NIV) - I remain confident of this: I will see the goodness of the LORD in the land of the living.

Chapter Two:

FULL SURRENDER

I went to college, and during the first semester of my freshman year, I was sexually assaulted the night after my 19th birthday. This was when I reached my breaking point; this just seemed like a reoccurring cycle in my life. I was tired of my life producing hurt; I was tired of running to everything and everyone to fulfill a void that they could never satisfy.

At this point, I turned back to God and cried out for help. Since my freshman year, God began to change my life around. Through the years, he has delivered and healed me. He has given me peace, love, and joy: something that no one can take away. God taught me how to forgive, and that's when I started to become free. After I forgave, I realized that the people that caused me pain, could have only been operating from their own personal hurt or insecurity, which allowed the enemy to use them and pervert their mind.

God was able to work in, and through me, when I surrendered. I began to grow an actual relationship with him, and have encounters and experiences with God for myself. Growing up in church, I knew of God, but I lacked a relationship with him. I heard about his healing power, but I never experienced it or believed it for myself. The church I grew up in focused more on fixing up the outward appearance of what they felt a Christian is "supposed" to look like, but as I grew up, I realized that holiness isn't a look, it was never supposed to be all about what I had on, but it was about what was on the inside.

1 Samuel 16:7(NIV) – But the Lord said to Samuel, Do not consider his appearance or his height, for I have rejected him. The Lord does not look at the things people look at. People look at the outward appearance, but the Lord looks at the heart.

Growing up, I was striving to look the part and be the part by acting like I had it all together, and the truth is I didn't, and it's okay because nobody does. I was attempting to do life in my own strength and my own way, and it only led to destruction. I had to give my life to Christ and commit my life to do his work. I had to understand that the imperfections I once hid on Sundays did not disqualify me from being used by God. God's best work and masterpieces start as broken pieces that he puts together so well. God's strength is truly made perfect in our weakness. God chose me, and he chose you too, and he has never changed his mind about us. So, you must let go of perception and trying to please people. You have to become a God pleaser and understand that God called, justifies, and glorifies you.

Romans 8:30(NIV) - And those he predestined, he also called; those he called, he also justified; those he justified, he also glorified.

Since then, my life hasn't been the same. After beginning my healing and walking into a better me, I realized that it was not going to be easy. Choosing to walk with God doesn't make life easier, but it makes you stronger. When you learn to trust God in every situation and cast your cares upon him, you will no longer be shaken by anything, because in his word, we believe that all things are working for our good even when we can't see or feel it.

Romans 8:17(NIV) - Now if we are children, then we are heirs—heirs of God and co-heirs with Christ if indeed we share in his sufferings so that we may also share in his glory.

Romans 8:28(KJV) - And we know that all things work together for good to them that love God, to them who are the called according to his purpose.

Sophomore year I had to adapt to overcome, and I was determined to grow even though. I had to adapt to this new way of living, and the seasons God brought me through. I had to allow God to detox me of my old ways so that I could walk in newness.

2 Corinthians 5:17(NIV) - Therefore, if anyone is in Christ, the new creation has come: The old has gone, the new is here!

I had to learn that my flesh will always be at war with my spirit man, which meant that I had to decide to die daily to my flesh and allow my spirit man to increase. Walking with God ultimately takes discipline. God doesn't remove trails and temptations; in times of trouble, we must choose him willingly by remaining steadfast, meaning loyal or faithful to God.

Psalms 51:10(NIV) - Create in me a pure heart, O God, and renew a steadfast spirit within me.

I was determined to grow because I refused to go back to the broken person I once was. When I was broken, I not only hurt me, but I also hurt, mistreated, and mishandled others. I was determined to be healed and whole, and I understood that Jesus was the only one who could do that in my life. When you choose to heal, you have to allow God to show you yourself, and this is not always delighting. Sometimes God pushes you to revisit times in your past so that you can heal from them.

Healing starts with forgiveness for those who caused you pain. Not only should you forgive them, but you also have to forgive yourself for making wrong choices, allowing yourself to settle for things you didn't deserve, and self-inflicted harm you caused. Do not hold yourself hostage, remember you have the keys to unlock and access your destiny. You have the power not to let your past and pains determine your future. You have to give yourself grace and be patient with your healing, it is not something that happens overnight; it takes time, but it's worth it. I was determined to grow despite what situation came my way. I took it as an opportunity to persevere and increase my faith. I saw it as an opportunity just to become wiser and better because I know that it is only preparing me for greater heights.

Junior year I survived a season called "was," this year, I began to reflect on my growth.

I was no longer hurt, but I am healed.

I was no longer broken, but I am beautifully and wonderfully made.

I was no longer lost, but I found my identity in Christ.

I was no longer angry, but I learned how to forgive and love despite the pain.

I was no longer going to let my past handicap my future.

I was no longer going to settle for less than what I deserved.

I was no longer stuck in religion, but I have a growing relationship with God.

I was no longer going to call on God for convenience, but I have a consistent spiritual walk with my heavenly father, and I learned to thank him in good times and bad and to thank him for the everyday blessings that we can sometimes take for granted.

Philippians 4:12(NIV) - I know what it is to be in need, and I know what it is to have plenty. I have learned the secret of being content in any and every situation, whether well fed or hungry, whether living in plenty or in want.

God transformed my life, and through it all, I never lost my praise. I experienced growing pains; I went through stages of isolation, rejection, heartbreak, and endured through tests and trails. Growing in God is never comfortable, but it works for your good.

I suffered from always trying to please people because I cared about the perception they had of me. God has blessed me so much and has allowed me to walk in freedom from people. He snatched me out of the enemy's hand, and he kept me even when I didn't want to be kept. When I wanted to let go, he kept his hand on me because his purpose was pulling me through. After I found and owned my identity in Christ, he gave me clarity and direction for my purpose.

When you choose to live for Christ, not everyone will or can support you because they may not understand. But this is a decision that you must make on your own and understand that everyone is not equipped to walk with you on your journey. Whoever you are attached to can ultimately determine how far you go or how much you will be held back. The people that were okay with you operating in hurt, will not be able to accept and support your transformation because they are still holding on to the old version of you. You didn't switch up or start acting differently; you just became a better version of yourself.

So, prepare for moments that feel like isolation, prepare for people to leave you, prepare for insults, feelings of being misunderstood, and feelings of being ostracized. God already warns us in his word that you may experience persecution for doing right and living for him. I have realized that trying to avoid persecution is the very thing that can hold people back from serving God wholeheartedly and speaking his truth. Pray for those who offend you and forgive them for yourself, whatever you do, don't give up and stay in position so you won't miss your harvest.

Matthew 5:10-12(NLT) - God blesses those who are persecuted for doing right, for the Kingdom of Heaven is theirs. God blesses you when people mock you and persecute you and lie about you and say all sorts of evil things against you because you are my followers. Be happy about it! Be very glad! For a great reward awaits you in heaven. And remember, the ancient prophets were persecuted in the same way.

Galatians 6:9(NLT) - So let's not get tired of doing what is good. At just the right time, we will reap a harvest of blessing if we don't give up.

You must believe and accept that you were not made to fit in, but God has called you to be set apart, but do not allow fear of being alone, dim your light. Do not allow the feeling of being alone and being the black sheep of the family to discourage you from your decision. But you must walk boldly and confidently.

Deuteronomy 7:6(NIV) - for you are a people holy to the Lord your God. Out of all the peoples on the face of the earth, the Lord has chosen you to be his treasured possession.

1 Peter 2:9(NIV) - But you are a chosen people, a royal priesthood, a holy nation, God's special possession, that you may declare the praises of him who called you out of darkness into his wonderful light.

I understand that my walk and fight is not just for me, but God is going to get the glory out of my life. There are souls attached to my obedience and yes to God. I have become a touchpoint for God to get what he desires to do through me and with me. God is not forceful, so you must have a willing heart to want to be transformed and used.

Now God has broken cycles in my life; he has broken soul ties, chains, and strongholds like fear and shame that held me in bondage for so long. All because I said yes to him, and I allowed him to operate on my life and my heart. He changed me and made me a new creature in him. He worked on me from the inside out. I am a generational curse breaker. I went from religion to relationship with God, and the Holy Spirit has manifested himself in my life. And now, because of my faith, I have the power to move mountains.

Matthew 17:20(NIV) – He replied, "Because you have so little faith. Truly I tell you, if you have faith as small as a mustard seed, you can say to this mountain, 'Move from here to there,' and it will move. Nothing will be impossible for you.

I've realized that God's goal was not only for me to be saved, but he ultimately wanted me to get in position to become so that he could use me to lead others. God is a strategic and intentional God, trust His plan, and trust the process even when it hurts, or you don't understand. My prayer life has increased, and I love reading

God's word, and I meditate on it daily, because it reads me, convicts me, changes me, and guides me in every aspect of my life.

> *Psalms 1:1-2(NIV) - Blessed is the one who does not walk in step with the wicked or stand in the way that sinners take or sit in the company of mockers, but whose delight is in the law of the Lord, and who meditates on his law day and night.*

God healed and set me free, God has my heart, and now I love me and value myself. Anytime that I feel discouraged, unqualified, or unworthy, I read God's word, and it reminds me of how highly my heavenly father speaks of me. Now I can love others with the love of God. I don't let people treat me anyway because I know who I am, I won't settle for less because I know who I am. Now I have purpose, and I see that there was a purpose for my pain. I am a willing vessel for God to use. I am the generational curse breaker of alcoholism, religion with no relationship, and a poverty mindset. I am no longer a slave to sexual immorality, fear, insecurities, pain, unforgiveness, or addiction to pornography.

I am totally and fully committed to God! I worship God in spirit and in truth. I am a walking, living, breathing testimony. My walk hasn't been perfect. I fell so many times and even still till this day, but because of God's love and grace, he forgives me, and I get back up each and every time, and God's mercy allows me to have another chance to do it right.

Romans 3:23(NIV) - for all have sinned and fall short of the glory of God.
Proverbs 24:16(NIV) - for though the righteous fall seven times, they rise again, the wicked stumble when calamity strikes.

So, this book is to encourage you to understand that the same grace of God is available to you. You don't have to have your whole life together, you don't have to wear certain clothes, God just wants your heart and for you to depend on him as your provider. My yes and coming into the truth about God; saved my life. God is a promise keeper and a way maker. I can't tell you my life story without telling you who God is. God does not want his children to be just "getting by," he has promised an abundant life. God doesn't just want you to survive; he wants you to thrive.

Just remember everything that the devil meant for evil, God has worked it out for your good! The same God who has performed miracles and raised from the dead is the same God who still lives today, and he is waiting for you to allow him in those places that lie dormant in your heart. Those daddy issues we all have, those insecurities, mental health issues, church hurt, hurt from abuse, heartbreak, divorce, hurt from family, grief, and even your deepest secrets you don't speak about. God wants you to come to him and be healed and set free. You do not have to be anyone else but yourself. God cannot work with something you pretend to be. God knows you, and he knows what you need before you ask.

God can save you from yourself. Those who have hurt you, left you, counted you out, and caused your pain is only responsible for the pain they caused you; you are responsible for your healing.

God waited on me, and he can do the same for you. Make yourself available for change, allow God to rearrange your life, and let God rewrite your story. He is the author and finisher of your life; he knew you before you were formed in your mother's womb. He sent you here with a purpose to be fulfilled, no matter what life has thrown at you, no matter where you come from, what you've been through, how far you feel away from God believe that God still has a plan for you, you are still useful to God.

> *Jeremiah 1:5(NIV) - Before I formed you in the womb, I knew you before you were born, I set you apart; I appointed you as a prophet to the nations. Galatians 1:15(NIV) - But when God, who set me apart from my mother's womb and called me by his grace, was pleased.*
> *Hebrews 12:2(NLT) - We do this by keeping our eyes on Jesus, the champion who initiates and perfects our faith. Because of the joy awaiting him, he endured the cross, disregarding its shame. Now he is seated in the place of honor beside God's throne.*

By walking with God, you learn to trust him more. Your walk will not be perfect, because if it were, you would no longer need God. God wants to be in partnership with you, and he will always come through even when you fall short. God is a forgiving God, and nothing separates us from his love for us. When the pressure of life came, hurt, pain, and fear were in me, so that's what came out of me. When I gave my pain to God through prayer and praise, it birthed my purpose. I pray that you will allow God to do the same for you.

Part Two:

RELIGION TO RELATIONSHIP

Chapter Three

WHAT IS A RELATIONSHIP?

A relationship is a way in which two or more people are connected. When I think of a relationship, I think of love, trust, and having a bond or connection with someone that I would do anything for because I value them. God desires to have a relationship with you. He wants you to get to know him intimately. Likewise, he desires for you to trust him and depend on him to supply all your needs. Also, he wants to hear from you daily, spend time with you, and help you to achieve a purpose-filled life. Once you embrace a relationship with him, your desire will then become to please him with your life. God's main focus is not for you to do things for him; he wants you to do things with him!

When walking with God, we should ultimately be aiming to be imitations or representations of him on earth. God is concerned about your motive and the position of your heart. God doesn't want forced obedience or sacrifice; he honors wholehearted and full obedience. Once God has your heart, he can transform you. Religion would force you to think that you have to get it right before you can get with God. However, God doesn't require you to be perfect; he just wants someone willing to progress. He wants you to depend on him and seek his guidance in everything you do.

When walking with God, everything you do should be led by him. We should aim to do things with his mindset, his love, and with a forgiving heart. We don't only have to worship God with song and praise in the four walls of the church, but God wants to equip us to be the church. He wants us to worship him with our lives, by putting on the full armor of God and putting what we have learned into practice.

John 4:23-24(TPT) - From here on, worshiping the Father will not be a matter of the right place but with the right heart. For God is a Spirit, and he longs to have sincere worshipers who worship and adore him in the realm of the Spirit and in truth.

Philippians 4:9(NIV) - Whatever you have learned or received or heard from me or seen in me —put it into practice. And the God of peace will be with you.

YOU HAVE TO BE WILLING

Growing up in church, I was doing things for God because I was told to, not because I was willing. I was taught a way that I should live, but never given the tools to navigate through life with its ups and downs.

I had a stereotyped look of holiness. There were certain things and places I was instructed not to go. But those were rules that were made up as a sacrifice. However, it had nothing to do with my obedience to God. My heart was still hardened. I was angry, broken, and selfish. I had impure thoughts, and so much more. I knew God, and I was involved in the things of God, but my heart was far from him. I was doing things in his name, considering myself a follower of Christ, but the more I started reading God's word, the more I noticed that there are true and false disciples. The position I once assumed, is one that God would say, depart from me, I never knew you.

A disciple is a personal follower of Christ. To follow Christ, you must know him by growing a relationship with him. How can you follow someone you don't take time to know? To follow Christ, you must know his character, and the only way you can learn that is through his word and persistently seeking him. I realized that I wanted to stop playing church, and actually become the devoted disciple God requires.

> *Matthew 7:21-23(NIV) - "Not everyone who says to me, 'Lord, Lord,' will enter the kingdom of heaven, but only the one who does the will of my Father who is in heaven. Many will say to me on that day, 'Lord, Lord, did we not prophesy in your name and in your name drive out demons and in your name perform many miracles?' Then I will tell them plainly, 'I never knew you. Away from me, you evildoers!'*

For me to change my habits, I had to give God my heart so he could change me from the inside out. I had to set my mind and treasure in God, and my heart followed.

> *Matthew 6:21(NIV) - For where your treasure is, there your heart will also be.*

A sacrifice always involves a choice of the person who decided to say no to themselves. However, obedience is saying yes to God and doing what he says with a good attitude. A good attitude is important because sometimes, in relationships with people, we can feel like we are doing so much for them that our pride could make us feel like we are doing them a favor.

With God, you have to want to be there because you love him, not because you think he needs you. When moving from religion to relationship with God, I realized that God was not just pleased with me attending service and performing religious activities and routines without my heart in it. I used to read his word like a history book, something that was only relevant in the past. However, his word is considered the "living" word of God, and it never changes. His word is a study guide for us to apply what we learn into our daily lives so that when the tests of life come, we would triumph.

God desires full transformation, and that comes with growing a relationship with him and not just being a Christian. More so, it goes beyond living life stagnant at salvation but for living deeper than being saved and putting his word into practice. God wants you to know his word, believe his word, and allow the word to come alive in you. When growing a relationship with God, and developing spiritually, I had to unlearn my old ways to become and learn who God called me to be. I had to allow God to renew my mind by letting go of old doctrines, misconceptions, and habits. I allowed God to do a new thing. When you give God your heart and seek him for clarity on your purpose, he will direct your paths.

Romans 12:2(NIV) - Do not conform to the pattern of this world but be transformed by the renewing of your mind. Then you will be able to test and approve what God's will is—his good, pleasing, and perfect will.

Proverbs 3:5-6(NIV) - Trust in the Lord with all your heart and lean not on your own understanding; in all your ways submit to him, and he will make your paths straight.

Chapter Four :

WHAT TO EXPECT

This Relationship with God will expose you to yourself

When you embrace a relationship with God, it will cause you to self-reflect. Subsequently, God will show you the things that you need to change to be in a position to prosper and live a life pleasing unto him. The great thing about it is that God does not expect you to transform alone. He will detox you of negative habits and mindsets and correct your wrong choices along the way. When you allow the Holy Spirit access, you will be able to bear the fruits of the Spirit, which are all opposite of what our flesh and what the world has caused us to produce. One thing God allowed me to see about myself is the position of my heart in different situations I faced.

His word said that we could do many things in life, for God, and people, but without love, it means nothing to him. His word further describes it as a *"resounding gong or a clanging cymbal."* God is love, and until you know him, you may think you have love all figured out. However, God brings us the truth about love. Without God, we can only depend on what the world and life situations have taught us. 1 Corinthians 13 defines God's love as perfect love.

> *1 Corinthians 13:13(NIV) - And now these three remain: faith, hope, and love. But the greatest of these is love.*

God allowed me to see that I needed a heart transplant, and the change had to start from within for me to heal and be a representation of him. *"And they will know we are Christians by our love,"* this was a memorable song I sang growing up in the church. God enabled me to realize that I could not love myself or anyone else properly until I accepted his love and allowed him to do surgery on my heart. We have all been hurt, offended, mistreated, rejected, broken, and misunderstood. Thus, to do God's work, you must deal with the unforgiveness, issues, and pain that we hold in our hearts.

> *Mark 12:30-31(NIV) - Love the Lord your God with all your heart and with all your soul and with all your mind and with all your strength. The second*

is this: 'Love your neighbor as yourself.' There is no commandment greater than these.

God's word also commands us to love others as ourselves. Personally, I began to realize that I didn't even love myself, so how could I love others properly? I did not love myself because my mind was clouded with guilt, shame, unworthiness, self-doubt, fear, insecurities, and depression. Accepting God's love allowed me to see that I no longer had to exist and suffer. With God's healing power, I could actually live a life and be whole.

Embracing a relationship with God allowed me to be real, honest, and transparent about the pain that I tried to hide for so long. With God, I no longer had to fake my happiness; God dealt with and healed me from a pain that seemed so unbearable that I wanted to end my life. Also, God allowed me to see that there was something still worth living for. The dreams and plans I once imagined were still possible. God opened my eyes to see that when I was hurt, I invariably hurt other people along the way because I had open wounds that I tried to cover up with a band-aid or temporary fixes.

When I released all my pain, my deepest fears, stress, and problems to God, he was able to heal me and give me everlasting love, peace, and joy, something I always heard about in church, but I had never experienced. The moment you have an authentic encounter with the Father, and you began to witness and experience his power, then you will be able to increase your faith and belief in him.

God also dealt with one of my root issues; my church hurt. When people come to church, they have a misconception that everything about it and within it will be perfect. When we are offended, let down, hurt, abused, judged, and mishandled by people, we take that pain and give up on God altogether. As soon as I released those that hurt me, I was able to forgive them without using the excuse to wait for an apology that was never coming.

Forgiveness is always for you and never for the person that offended you. After I forgave, I was able to try God again and even repent for giving up on Him. This taught me not to put high expectations in people any longer. I learned to ultimately put my trust in God because he will never let me down. God healed me and changed my mindset, and then he gave me another church that I could appreciate. While embracing my new church, he taught me how to keep my eyes on him alone. Therefore, if you have been asking God to do a new thing in your life while still holding on to an old mindset, you will not be able to receive what God has for you. Sometimes our mindset or grudges we hold can delay the process. I learned that the church is not supposed to be a perfect place. It is a place of fellowship for the people and believers that have acknowledged that they need God. The church is like a hospital, and many come for different reasons, issues, or concerns.

Note that the purpose of attending church isn't to stay sick and remain comfortable in sin. The goal is for you to be restored and made whole. Also, it is for you to walk in freedom and full deliverance. That's why in a church, you need a pastor that leads by example, nurtures, and builds you to become what God has called you to be. The pastor should not be seen or used as a crutch; the pastor's job is to teach you how to approach God for yourself. Some want to be leaders and have the title, but are not good examples to follow.

Also, I had to understand the difference between God and man. God has become the source of my life, and so no matter what happens, he has instructed and taught me how to fight and stand on His word. This relationship with Christ is worth fighting for; he is so loving and selfless. He paid the ultimate sacrifice for the world so that we can be saved. I encourage you to give yourself to Christ as a living sacrifice by fully committing yourself to him, and His will for your life.

Romans 12:1(NIV) – Therefore, I urge you, brothers, and sisters, in view of God's mercy, to offer your bodies as a living sacrifice, holy and pleasing to God—this is your true and proper worship.
John 3:16(KJV) – For God so loved the world, that he gave his only begotten Son, that whosoever believeth in him should not perish, but have everlasting life.

Throughout my walk with Christ, he has revealed me to myself a lot of times. However, I will only highlight a few more points that changed my life forever.

OVERCOMING FEAR

Apart from revealing my true self to me, God also dealt with my fear of rejection and failure. There were many things I settled for due to fear of rejection. There were many things I never did or hesitated to start due to the fear of failure. I lived my life in fear of the unknown and "what if's." Instead of stepping out on faith and speaking positively about what it "will be," I had to take the limits off of what I believed God could do in my life. I learned how to confront my fears, and even if I still had unbelief, I did it afraid.

OVERCOMING THE URGE FOR "SELF-COMPARISON"

Also, God dealt with my problem of comparing myself to others. When you compare yourself to others, you can end up trying to walk in a lane, at a pace, and following instructions that were never designed for you. Comparison kills purpose and confidence. God gives gifts, talents, and wisdom according to your abilities. We must learn to work with and value what he gives us because when you value your gift from God, you will use it wisely.

This leads to the Parable of the Talents in Matthew 25:14-30. A parable is a simple story that is used to illustrate a moral or spiritual lesson. In this particular parable, three servants were gifted different talents from their master. One, he gave five talents, the other three, and the other one. The two men that had five and three talents both worked with what they had and was able to multiply and made a profit. The one that was given one talent dug a hole in the ground and hid his gift. The two men who multiplied what was given to them received a well done from the master. The master rewarded them with more because they were faithful over the little, so that they could be trusted with more. The other servant that hid his one talent came up with an excuse. He feared losing the gift or that it would fail because it couldn't produce the expected result. The master called him a wicked and lazy servant. Here, the servant let the fear of failure and loss, hinder him from producing. The master didn't judge the other two servants differently because one had more than the other. It's not about what you have compared to everyone else. It's about what you do with what God entrusted you with. When you focus on others, the enemy and your flesh can allow you to be jealous, covet, and envy others. Remember that is something God instructs us not to do. While you are coveting another person's blessing, or their work ethic, or their talent or gift, you are missing out on what God has given you.

> *2 Corinthians 10:12(NIV) - We do not dare to classify or compare ourselves with some who commend themselves. When they measure themselves by themselves and compare themselves with themselves, they are not wise.*
> *Galatians 5:26(NIV) - Let us not become conceited, provoking, and envying each other.*
> *James 3:16(NIV) - For where you have envy and selfish ambition, there you will find disorder and every evil practice.*

FOLLOW THE INSTRUCTION WHOLEHEARTEDLY

In your walk with God, you must stay focused on the explicit instructions he has given you to prosper in your lane. You will only be able to respond to his instructions if you have an ongoing relationship with God. That enables you to recognize His voice when He is talking to you. Just like when we spend time around the same person long enough, naturally, we are able to pick up how they sound because it becomes familiar to us. Likewise, allow God's voice to become familiar to you. He meets us where we are regardless. Thus, you cannot compare your process or journey to anyone else. You must learn to become confident in who God has called you to be.

Sometimes when we focus on what we don't have and take for granted what we do, we miss out on the great things God has for us in that particular season.

Remember, God calls us by name, and he has plans for every one of us. Therefore, we must trust his timing and the process. Therefore, we must be able to rejoice for others. Use it as encouragement that if God could do it for them, then he can come through for you too.

Also, we must be careful when asking God for some-things. God has many reasons for saying wait or no. Often, you may not be ready for what you are asking. God's no or wait is always for your protection. Many times, I have questioned, "Why is God making me wait?" However, I have realized that we can't always bear all we ask from him. Sometimes his "No" is to protect you from touching things or releasing things prematurely and out of season. When you operate out of season, you will never get the expected result. Just like you wouldn't expect it to snow in the summer naturally or leaves to grow on trees in the winter. Likewise, understanding and surrendering yourself to God's timing of things is crucial because when he says, "Go," you have the assurance that it will prosper.

Besides, God is all-knowing, and sometimes him being with us, is all the guarantee that we need. You don't have to have it all figured out for you to go or be obedient to the all-knowing God we serve. There were times I asked God for answers that he made me wait for. But because I was so close-minded and focused on what I wanted to hear; I was oblivious to what he actually was letting me know at that time. The testing of our faith builds endurance and trust in God. Another reason he may say "wait or no" is if we are asking for things out of our own pleasure. Remember, God examines the heart.

James 4:3(NIV) - When you ask, you do not receive, because you ask with wrong motives, that you may spend what you get on your pleasures.

With God, you will learn how to overcome disappointment and frustration. This is because if you trust Him as your source, you can believe that all things are still working together for your good even when you don't understand. Eventually, it will all make sense. My relationship with God allowed me to become selfless, free, forgiving, and loving. This is a version of myself I had to get used to and ultimately grow to be proud of. There was also a version of me that people didn't always recognize. Therefore, anytime something or someone comes to remind you of your past, remember that you are a new creature and do not let anything or anyone take you, keep you, or deter you from the promises of God.

This relationship will help you change your mindset about you

In the presence of God, you can denounce all the labels, all the negative things that were put on you, and still try to haunt you to this day. The thoughts that were birthed from abuse, abandonment, bullying, feeling overlooked, and maltreatment can all be erased when you accept the love God has for you. His love is always perfect.

Embracing a relationship with God allows you to know the truth about you in his word. Everything you need is in God. When you find your identity in Christ, and own who and whose you are, you become unstoppable. So, when you are feeling alone, afraid, or misunderstood, remember that His word tells us to be courageous because God will always be with us. Even when you feel like you can't trace or feel God, He is there. When you learn to trust God fully, you gain a sense of security. *Affirmation: I am not alone; God is with me.*

Joshua 1:9 (NLT) - This is my command—be strong and courageous! Do not be afraid or discouraged. For the Lord, your God is with you wherever you go.

Whenever you feel like you have made a mistake, or when you sin, and you are close to giving up due to feelings of unworthiness or out of the belief that God is mad at you and you are no longer useful. Focus on His word that tells us that we are forgiven. He still loves us despite our messy condition. The moment you feel like your imperfections disqualify you, God reminds you that he can do much with what you allow him to have access to. God is able to turn your mess into a message and work a miracle in your life. *Affirmation: I am not condemned, I am forgiven and set free from shame and guilt.*

1 John 2:12(NIV) - I am writing to you, dear children, because your sins have been forgiven on account of his name.

> *Romans 8:1(KJV) - There is therefore now no condemnation to them which are in Christ Jesus, who walk not after the flesh, but after the Spirit.*

When we are feeling weak, His word tells us to rejoice in these times because his strength is made perfect in our weaknesses. When we come in partnership with God, he is able to pick us up and bring us through. Sometimes when in a relationship with man, the test of real friendship, love, or loyalty is to see if they will remain, whether good or bad.

God is with you at all times. He will never leave you because there is nothing too hard for him, and he is a promise keeper. He is all-knowing, and he is in control. You must allow yourself to release your problems and needs to God, instead of venting out, vent up to God who has the power to transform your situation. God can turn your test or trial into a testimony. I have learned to take every test or trial as a character-building opportunity and a learning experience. God brought you to it so that he can get you through it. *Affirmation: When I am weak, I am made strong.*

2 Corinthians 12:8-10(NKJV) - Concerning this thing, I pleaded with the Lord three times that it might depart from me. And He said to me, "My grace is sufficient for you, for My strength is made perfect in weakness." Therefore, most gladly, I will rather boast in my infirmities, that the power of Christ may rest upon me. Therefore, I take pleasure in infirmities, in reproaches, in needs, in persecutions, in distresses, for Christ's sake. For when I am weak, then I am strong.

God helps you to overcome obstacles instead of trying to find a way around them. God allows us to become conquerors by helping us to face the problem. With God, you can overcome addiction, impurity, depression, loss, heartbreak, whatever else that seems to hold you down. Some suffer from these issues in silence in fear of being judged, even believers that attend church regularly. This is because somewhere along the way, they were never taught how to overcome. When they attempted to overcome in their own strength and failed, they gave up and allowed it to become a part of their identity. In life, the temptation will come, and weapons may form against you, but they will not prosper; God has given you the power to overcome. *Affirmation: I shall never be defeated, I am an overcomer.*

Isaiah 54:17(KJV) - No weapon that is formed against thee shall prosper, and every tongue that shall rise against thee in judgment thou shalt condemn. This is the heritage of the servants of the Lord, and their righteousness is of me, saith the Lord.

1 John 4:4(NLT) - But you belong to God, my dear children. You have already won a victory over those people because the Spirit who lives in you is greater than the Spirit who lives in the world.

Romans 8:31-33(NIV) - What, then, shall we say in response to these things? If God is for us, who can be against us? He who did not spare his own Son but gave him up for us all—how will he not also, along with him, graciously give us all things? Who will bring any charge against those whom God has chosen? It is God who justifies.

YOU ARE WORTH IT

One thing that I struggled with affirming and believing for myself is that I was worth it. I struggled with self-worth and the need to be justified by others. I struggled with self-worth because I was ashamed of how careless I was with my body at one point in my life. At one point, I used to believe that was all I was good for or worth. I was ashamed of my past and my poor decisions. My lack of self-worth affected the way I treated myself and the way I allowed others to treat me. But Christ's sacrifice on the cross reminds us that he thought we were worth dying for. *Affirmation: I am worth it, I am special, and I am enough.*

John 3:16(NIV) – For God so loved the world that he gave his one and only Son, that whoever believes in him shall not perish but have eternal life.

God grants us a peace-filled life. So, when you feel like life has gotten chaotic, and you believe that you have lost control, you can declare peace over the situation. God's word makes a clear distinction between his peace and the peace of the world. God's peace is perfect and everlasting, while the peace of the world is only temporary. For so long, I found myself looking for a sense of peace or comfort in everything but God. Sometimes, I even thought that I needed God and the substance to have peace. Some things we may turn to could be drugs or other substances such as alcohol, sage, overeating, sex, or even people. It could be anything that we use to temporarily fix how we are feeling or to "keep ourselves together."

We use these things to control, hide, or numb our feelings momentarily. These things that we turn to can be a weight that slows our walk with Christ down because we often began to put these things before Christ. God is all you need, so the next time you feel like you need peace, go to God first! *Affirmation: I am peace-filled by God, my mind stays at peace.*

John 14:27(NIV) - Peace I leave with you; my peace I give you. I do not give to you as the world gives. Do not let your hearts be troubled and do not be afraid.

Sometimes we may struggle with believing that God has plans for us. Sometimes situations arise, and they look or seem bigger than our God. We must remember who we put our trust in and believe that God honors his word. Sometimes when we face struggles or adversities on our walk with Christ, we began to doubt the plan he has to prosper us. But, we must remember that God has an appointed time for everything. His promises require a process and obedience. Don't allow God to waste his breath of life on you; don't be wasted potential! Trust His process and rest in his promises for your life. Everything God makes is for a purpose, and it shall be fulfilled. *Affirmation: With God, I have a purpose to prosper; I already have the victory!*

Isaiah 55:11(NIV) - so is my word that goes out from my mouth: It will not return to me empty but will accomplish what I desire and achieve the purpose for which I sent it.

In this relationship, you will experience perfect love, his love makes you whole.

> *1 John 4:18(NIV) – There is no fear in love. But perfect love drives out fear because fear has to do with punishment. The one who fears is not made perfect in love.*

To walk confidently in your calling and purpose, fear must be eliminated. Fear can no longer control you, but you must activate your power over it. Experiencing God's perfect love will cast out all fear. Fear has to do with punishment. Some people are afraid of love because they have been hurt or betrayed by those who claimed to love them. Those who fear and can't accept real love will always think they can't trust it, or it's too good to be true. They anticipate the worst to happen, and consequently, they fear the punishment or result of love. When you carry around hurt, you won't be able to see or receive real love.

You must change your mindset and receive God's perfect love first; his love is unfailing and unconditional. God's love is real; he cares for you and has your best interest at heart. He has allowed me to understand and learn the difference between feeling lonely and being alone. God deals with the most inner parts of us and allows us to operate from a place of wholeness and confidence. God has taught me how to embrace my singleness and renounce the thoughts that come to tell me I am lonely. Loneliness comes with a feeling of sadness that you are by yourself. Consequently, this feeling can allow you to believe the lies of the enemy that will cause you to rush and deny the season of life you are in.

Loneliness can then turn into a desperation where you will fight to be loved and accepted by those who have not been able to love themselves properly. Loneliness and desperation are vulnerable places where the enemy can then present you with things to compromise or try to operate out of season. You will begin to trust and accept anyone into your life even after they hurt you repeatedly with no effort to change. You will settle and stay in places that hurt you while acknowledging that it is normal. The truth is you deserve better! You will even force relationships and friendships that were never meant to be. You will surround yourself with so many people that don't even deserve you just because you long for the company. You will surround yourself with people that leave you drained and don't even know who you truly are. When you are lonely and not whole, you will attract what you are, and it will just be two half-empty people trying to love one another. Instead of pouring into each other and growing, you began to bruise each other even more.

God allows you to become content in the season he has allocated for you. He enables you to become okay with being alone; he sustains you. God's plan for your life is already written, and it's perfect, we may not always understand because his thoughts are not like ours. God has shown me that there is a purpose in waiting. I have learned to embrace seasons of singleness, isolation, and even being heartbroken and rejected. There is a reason for everything, and once you realize that there are no losses in God, you can only forgo things for God to do his will. Even when you are hurt by the people that leave you, you learn to understand that it had to happen that way.

Also, understand that a break-up hardly ends well. It's a situation where it hurts to leave, but it causes so much more pain to stay. I have learned to trust the process and trust that great things take time. In the moments where you feel like you are waiting, ask God to help you to be steadfast. Sometimes waiting can began to feel like a weight. Waiting won't feel like a burden if you have good posture, trust, and expectancy in God. Ask God to show you the good amid something you feel is testing your faith. Ask God to show you yourself in the situation. Most situations that frustrated and hurt me at first always leaves me with wisdom and knowledge. I learned to trust God more and seek him in everything. The wait prepares you for what God has for you. Don't lose out on what you need, focusing on your preference, desires, lusts, and desperations at the time. Trust that God has you exactly where you need to be.

Isaiah 55:8-9(NIV) - For my thoughts are not your thoughts, neither are your ways my ways, declares the Lord. As the heavens are higher than the earth, so are my ways higher than your ways and my thoughts than your thoughts.

DON'T IGNORE HIS FATHERLY CORRECTION

God's perfect love also corrects you. Correction sometimes hurts, but it is for your good. God has plans and promises for us, and he directs us on how to get there. God doesn't require us to be perfect, but to progress or grow in him you must have conviction. Conviction comes from the Holy Spirit. It convicts us of our wrongdoings. Conviction isn't wrong because it leads us back to God through repentance, and that makes us right with him. Personally, I have experienced conviction, and it felt like a deeply sorrowful and uneasy feeling in my Spirit. This was a feeling I had never felt before. Hence, at first, I attempted to ignore it, but it didn't seem to go away. Conviction is something you should not ignore because that is a way the Holy Spirit guides us. If you ignore conviction or correction, that births disobedience and subsequently leads to disappointment. The correction to change is always for your best interest. Your response to conviction should always be repentance. Repentance means that you are sorry, and you choose to turn away from that sin. It takes confession with the mouth and action to turn back to God.

Proverbs 3:12(NIV) - because the Lord disciplines those he loves, as a father the son he delights in.

Psalms 84:11(KJV) - For the Lord God is a sun and shield: the Lord will give grace and glory: no good thing will he withhold from them that walk uprightly.

In this relationship God listens and responds

God can only listen and respond to someone that talks and spends time with him. In God, you can find everything you need, but you must be willing to open your mouth and cast your cares upon him because he cares. You must wait, listen, and watch for his response. Prayer is how we communicate with God. God responds to those that diligently and persistently seek him in prayer. Prayer doesn't have seasons. It's something you must do without ceasing; it keeps you growing consistently.

Prayer sustains your walk with Christ, changes things, and produces results. When you pray, you must then believe that you have received whatever you asked. You can pray and ask God for anything, take your limits off God, and believe in his power. God's ears are open to those that do right, obey, and please him. God will give you whatever you ask for according to his will.

We must be like Jesus when he prayed in the garden of Gethsemane. You have to align your heart to do God's will above your own. Prayer is the place where our will has to align with his. Through prayer, we come into agreement with God's will. Everything we may want may not be good for us or may not be for the appointed time. It is so imperative to ask and seek God because his will always prevails.

> *Luke 22:42(NLT) - Father, if you are willing, please take this cup of suffering away from me. Yet I want your will to be done, not mine.*
> *Luke 11:9-10(NIV) - So I say to you: Ask, and it will be given to you; seek and you will find; knock, and the door will be opened to you. For everyone who asks receives; the one who seeks finds; and to the one who knocks, the door will be opened.*
> *Mark 11:24(NIV) - Therefore I tell you, whatever you ask for in prayer, believe that you have received it, and it will be yours.*

After we ask or commit our life to God, we must then evaluate our response. Will you answer the call? Will you listen? Will you obey? Will you apply his wisdom? I have gotten to a point in my life where my position has become, "God whatever it takes, I'm all in." This is the stance that God desires because he wants to trust and see if we will obey to receive what he has for us. Prayer shouldn't just be a time we use to ask God for things. We must also honor and come to him with a heart full of gratitude for what he has already done.

Prayer is also a time to ask for forgiveness and help to forgive others. Pray for others as well because it's not all about you. Prayer is also a time to ask God to continue to help you, nurture, and grow you in your spiritual walk. There is no destination one reaches in their walk with Christ and become satisfied. You should always push to progress because no one is perfect. There are co-requisites for prayer, meaning there are other requirements you must be applying concurrently.

> *John 15:7(NIV) - If you remain in me and my words remain in you, ask whatever you wish, and it will be done for you.*

The definition of remain is to continue to exist, especially after other similar or related people or things have ceased. It means to stay, to endure, abide, and persist. God wants us to remain in him, and he wants his word to remain in us. For the word to remain in us, it must first be put there and consistently studied. For us to remain in him, we must continue to feed ourselves spiritually and strive to be better versions of ourselves. Remain committed even when other people may leave or fall astray.

You must have the word in you so that you can withstand anything that comes your way. This is why building your relationship with God is essential because when you experience and understand him for yourself, your commitment to him won't change based on people and circumstances. When communicating with God, he wants us to come boldly and confidently. Meaning without any feelings of unworthiness, doubt, shame, guilt, or low expectations. Give God the real you. As soon as you become consistent with communication with God, you realize your need for him. Consequently, you will never try to do things on your own anymore. When you stay in communication with God, you will begin to see things manifest in your life. When God blesses you, don't forget to give him the glory and the credit because without him, where would we be.

THE GIFT OF THE HOLY SPIRIT

John 3:5-6(NIV) - Jesus answered, Very truly I tell you, no one can enter the kingdom of God unless they are born of water and the Spirit. Flesh gives birth to flesh, but the Spirit gives birth to Spirit. Acts 2:38(KJV) - Then Peter said unto them, Repent, and be baptized every one of you in the name of Jesus Christ for the remission of sins, and ye shall receive the gift of the Holy Ghost.

The Holy Spirit is a gift for everyone God calls to himself. The gift of the Holy Spirit gives birth to our spiritual life. Growing up, I had many misconceptions about the Holy Spirit. First, I learned the difference between baptism and the Holy Spirit. Baptism symbolizes faith and committing oneself to God. It symbolizes the burial of old life and the resurrection of new life. The Holy Spirit isn't just for or given to a selected few; it is for all God's people. The Holy Spirit is a gift given to those whose heart is eager, hungry, open, and ready to receive. The Holy Spirit does not make you or your life perfect; it helps and leads you to progress in your spiritual walk.

> *John 3:34(NIV) - For the one whom God has sent speaks the words of God, for God gives the Spirit without limit.*
>
> *John 14:15-17(NIV) - If you love me, keep my commands. And I will ask the Father, and he will give you another advocate to help you and be with you forever— the Spirit of truth. The world cannot accept him because it neither sees him nor knows him. But you know him, for he lives with you and will be in you.*

Another misconception I had about the Holy Spirit is that it makes you perfect. The Spirit is an advocate, The Holy Spirit doesn't make you perfect; instead, it helps you to progress in your spiritual walk. There will be times when you are weak, and God will be there to make you strong. Sometimes we don't know what to pray for, so the Spirit will intercede for us.

> *Romans 8:26 (NIV) - In the same way, the Spirit helps us in our weakness. We do not know what we ought to pray for, but the Spirit himself intercedes for us through wordless groans.*

God gives us the Holy Spirit as a down payment. The Holy Spirit is confirmation of the promise of eternal life. The Holy Spirit is our seal of ownership.

2 Corinthians 1:21-22(NIV) - Now it is God who makes both us and you stand firm in Christ. He anointed us, set his seal of ownership on us, and put his Spirit in our hearts as a deposit, guaranteeing what is to come.
2 Corinthians 5:4-5(NIV) - For while we are in this tent, we groan and are burdened, because we do not wish to be unclothed but to be clothed instead with our heavenly dwelling so that what is mortal may be swallowed up by life. Now the one who has fashioned us for this very purpose is God, who has given us the Spirit as a deposit, guaranteeing what is to come.
2 Corinthians 5:14-15(NIV) - For Christ's love compels us because we are convinced that one died for all, and therefore all died. And he died for all, that those who live should no longer live for themselves but for him who died for them and was raised again.

Christ died for us; now, we must die daily to ourselves and allow Christ to live through us. You are no longer self-ambitious and doing things to please yourself and your flesh. You are living a life controlled by God. Your passion becomes living a life pleasing unto him. Allow God to get the glory out of your life. You need the Holy Spirit because that is the only way you will be

able to operate in Spirit. You need the Spirit to understand God fully. You need the Spirit to guide you; the
Spirit knows the thoughts of God.

> *1 Corinthians 2:11(NLT) - No one can know a
> person's thoughts except that person's own Spirit,
> and no one can know God's thoughts except God's
> own Spirit.*
> *1 Corinthians 2:14(NLT) - But people who aren't
> spiritual can't receive these truths from God's
> Spirit. It all sounds foolish to them, and they can't
> understand it, for only those who are spiritual can
> understand what the Spirit means.*
> *Romans 8:9(NLT) - But you are not controlled by
> your sinful nature. You are controlled by the Spirit
> if you have the Spirit of God living in you. (And
> remember that those who do not have the Spirit of
> Christ living in them do not belong to him at all.)*

You must become a spiritual being to be able to do
what God has called you to do. God instructs us to operate in Spirit and be not of the flesh. The Spirit of God
living inside of you allows you to live a life pleasing
unto God. It's not all about what you do for God in your
works. God has to be on the throne of your heart, and
you must abide in him. The Holy Spirit allows the fruit
of the Spirit to be manifested. The Holy Spirit allows
you to walk in full freedom that you no longer live under
the domination of the law and your old life, but you soar
above it. Everything connected to your old self was put

to death on the cross and crucified. For something to resurrect, it first has to die.

Walking in the Spirit takes action and effort. You must choose to follow the Spirit and not your flesh because they will always be at war with each other. That's why it seems hard sometimes when you try to do good and be good, and you feel like evil is always present. You must remember that you can have the Holy Spirit, but it is still wrapped and dwells in our fleshly bodies, and in our flesh dwells no good thing.

> *Romans 7:15-20(NIV) - I do not understand what I do. For what I want to do, I do not do, but what I hate I do. And if I do what I do not want to do, I agree that the law is good. As it is, it is no longer I myself who do it, but it's sin living in me. I know that good itself does not dwell in me, that is, in my sinful nature. For I have the desire to do what is good, but I cannot carry it out. For I do not do the good, I want to do, but the evil I do not want to do—this I keep on doing. Now if I do what I do not want to do, it is no longer I who do it, but it is a sin living in me that does it.*

God gives us free will, meaning he isn't a forceful God. Therefore, we must choose to do good or evil. We must decide to be obedient or disobedient. We must choose to follow Christ wholeheartedly. We must decide if we want a convenient or covenant relationship with

God. Just like we feed our natural bodies, we must feed our spirit man as well. Your Spirit can become stronger than your flesh and overrule it, which means, with the Spirit, birth self-control. You have control over your emotions, feelings, and actions.

You can feed your Spirit through reading God's word because what's in you will come out of you. You must submerge yourself with the things of God, so then you can operate with his mindset, and your actions will follow. You can also feed your Spirit with prayer and fasting. Growing up, I used to only fast when instructed, and I honestly never understood the purpose. I thought it was just a sacrifice made for God. You don't have to wait for someone to call a fast before you observe it, fasting should be a part of your spiritual walk and obedience to Christ. Fasting is denying your flesh for a spiritual gain and connection with God. Fasting is not to make you suffer; it should be accompanied by prayer. Fasting builds your focus and your awareness and makes you less self-centered. It provokes a move of God, when you fast do it with expectation.

In the Bible, fasting was done for the preparation of ministry. Jesus himself spent time fasting and praying for 40 days before he began to do God's work. You need time alone to prepare for what God has called you to do. Fasting is also observed to seek God's wisdom, repent, seek deliverance or protection, or to gain a victory. Fasting is spiritual, so do not expect a natural gain from it. Jesus gives instructions for fasting in Matthew 6.

> *Matthew 6: 17–18(NIV) - But when you fast, put oil on your head and wash your face, so that it will not be obvious to others that you are fasting, but only to your Father, who is unseen; and your Father, who sees what is done in secret, will reward you. Galatians 5:16(NIV) - So I say, walk by the Spirit, and you will not gratify the desires of the flesh.*

You can walk, pray, and live through the Holy Spirit as your guide. Thank God for the Holy Spirit, and never grieve His presence in your life.

Chapter Five:

A PUSH AWAY FROM COMFORT

This walk with God requires you to live beyond your comfort level. You will experience growing pains. Growing pains can be, having to say no to addiction, being different, misunderstood, or persecuted by family, friends, or peers. However, when you let go of trying to please people and just please God, you will understand that all you have to endure is worth it, and it's nothing compared to what God has for you.

Romans 8:18(KJV) - For I reckon that the sufferings of this present time are not worthy of being compared with the glory which shall be revealed in us.

God is going to push you to become a far better version of yourself you could not even imagine. God will birth things out of you that you never envisioned yourself doing. Writing this book is proof that God can birth great things in uncomfortable situations. Living life in sin can be comfortable and exciting for only a little while. When you began living for God you must leave those old habits, old friends, and old mindsets behind. Allow God to renew your mind so that your life will follow. Letting go of anything that you enjoy can be hard. You know it's time to let go when it hurts you more to stay.

Change, growth, and freedom don't feel good at first, but it's worth it. Growth and comfort can't mix. Don't allow your preference of comfortability to hinder you from growing, glowing, and receiving the blessings God has in store for you. It won't feel good because it's something you are not yet used to. But God's will for your life will begin to become your norm, and it will no longer seem hard. Some people are afraid to embrace a new life in Christ in fear of what they will have to give up or stop doing. Understand that when you first give your life to Christ you don't naturally stop or give up everything you used to do, the transformation occurs over time.

Once I began to live for God, my desires began to change. Subsequently, certain things like partying all the time and getting drunk were no longer fun to me. It ceased to be my norm. Indulging in pornography was no longer exciting because I became aware of the harm it causes. Suddenly, indulging in sex before marriage and sexual immorality no longer seemed worth it because I started to desire to have a pure mind and to wait for sex to be honorable before God. I began to want to forgive instead of holding grudges. I began to want God's will for my life more than my own, even when it hurt. I began to desire ways to get closer to God, the more.

I started enjoying serving in ministries at my church and on my college campus. I started embracing the fact that I was not made to fit in. I stopped hiding my zeal for God and stepped into my role as a Christ representative and ambassador. I became unashamed to speak the Gospel of Jesus Christ because I realized that God is someone everyone needs in their life. I stopped being ashamed because I knew that it was not just something that happened to me, but that He lives through me. I began to get comfortable in who God called me to be.

Once you know and can affirm your identity in Christ, the enemy and his lies can no longer have power over you. God allowed me to outgrow my comfort zone. He allowed me to see beyond the life I was living and ultimately want better for myself and those that followed. Remember, success and prosperity never come easy. You must put in the work on and off the scenes. Meaning, you must develop a relationship with God and not just hear his word, but to put it into practice. Worship him with your life.

This relationship is also uncomfortable because it requires you to deal with you and confront issues and weaknesses you once tried to hide. This relationship requires you to love and accept you and all that comes with it. Loving yourself can sometimes be hard, but once you began to see yourself how God sees you, you will be able to see and believe in your potential. I had a hard time loving myself because, for so long, I was striving to be perfect and fit this imaginary image of what a Christian looked and acted like. I wanted to be perfect for God, myself, and my parents. Whenever I made a mistake, I would live my life and operate out of shame and guilt. I would literally talk down on myself, and when you carry shame, you then began to believe the lie that you should just keep sinning because you already missed the mark.

I was the one that once used to see the worst in myself while God and others around me saw the best. I was the one that counted myself out of being able to accomplish things because I wanted to be perfect. I was very judgmental to myself, and I was holding myself to this exception of perfection that can never be achieved. I realized that the same way I treated myself, I began to treat others by being judgmental and always being able to point out the faults in people and ignoring mine. Sometimes you can even find the fault so easily in someone else because you struggle with the same sin.

Matthew 7:1-5(NIV) - Do not judge, or you too will be judged. For in the same way you judge others, you will be judged, and with the measure you use, it will be measured to you. "Why do you look at the speck of sawdust in your brother's eye and pay no attention to the plank in your own eye? How can you say to your brother, 'Let me take the speck out of your eye,' when all the time there is a plank in your own eye? You hypocrite! First, take the plank out of your own eye, and then you will see clearly to remove the speck from your brother's eye.

I got to a point in my life where I realized that I didn't want to be wasted potential. I wanted to see and believe in the version of me that God sees. You have to be willing to do all the work that it takes to get there. You can have faith and the belief that you can be changed, but actions will speak louder than words. Faith without work is dead. Sometimes we may feel as if our "faith in God" isn't working not realizing that we are the problem.

When you want anything in life, you set your mind to it and work hard and do whatever it takes to get it. It amazes me how sometimes when things get hard in our walk with God, we want to give up and throw in the towel. We must endure to the very end just like we do with other things in life. Things like finishing school, working at a job you may not even like, entrepreneurship, being in a relationship, being a parent. We stay in position because there is a reward at the end of a need being met.

The same way we hold on and endure through the problems that come with these things is the same mind-set we should adopt when walking with God. If you stop pushing and working in the middle, we will never get to see the promise. You may get weary, but don't faint. You may get tired, but keep pressing towards the mark and set your thoughts on things above. Everyone has a reason for the choices they make. When I get discouraged, I began to remember my why, that keeps me going. If you hold on to why and how you started, it will always be your motivation to keep going. You've come too far to give up now, what's in front of you is better than what's behind you.

Colossians 3:2-4(NIV) - Set your minds on things above, not on earthly things. For you died, and your life is now hidden with Christ in God. When Christ, who is your life, appears, then you also will appear with him in glory.
Philippians 3:13-14(NIV) - Brothers and sisters, I do not consider myself yet to have taken hold of it. But one thing I do: Forgetting what is behind and straining toward what is ahead, I press on toward the goal to win the prize for which God has called me heavenward in Christ Jesus.

Isaiah 43:19(NIV) - See, I am doing a new thing! Now it springs up; do you not perceive it? I am making a way in the wilderness and streams in the wasteland.

An uncomfortable season I believe everyone experiences is a "wilderness" moment in their walk with Christ. This season seems like a period of stagnation. It's that season where you can't see your way out. The wilderness is a place that is uncultivated, uninhabited, and an inhospitable region. It is a season where you feel like God, and everyone has neglected you. It's a season you may feel isolated, overlooked and hidden.

In the wilderness, you feel alone and that you must fend for yourself. Many may describe this season as the feeling of suffering, and all they are trying to do is survive and make it through. You can either fight or flight. This season is to help equip you with the things you need to survive and thrive in your walk with Christ. You being hidden is for protection of what's being developed. The wilderness is a place you go through in transition from your bondage to your promise. This season may make you feel like you should've stayed comfortable in your bondage and never embraced freedom, you must believe that the test wasn't meant to kill you; it was meant to build you. When you are representing God and living for him, he doesn't want you to be weak. Therefore, he has to build you so that when attack or trouble comes, you can remain standing.

In this season, you discover you, your abilities, your strengths, and your weaknesses. Just because you are facing trials, tests, and attacks does not mean God is not there. He allowed it to come to you so that he could bring you through it, and not for you to run from it. In the wilderness, you can see the best part of you, ask God to show you what he sees in you. The wilderness can be frustrating and uncomfortable because you lose control. God is now in control and determines how and when you will move. He will honor your obedience and your persistence in the wilderness. God's love for you will push you even if it's uncomfortable because, in the end, it's rewarding.

Some believers will disregard this season, but it's an important season because it tests your survival skills. When you are free from what you once knew, you must walk into newness by faith and be processed and developed, so you will be able to handle, receive, and enjoy what God has for you. In this season, ask God for endurance, strength, and perseverance. You have to allow your faith to develop fully and pray for perseverance to finish its work through you. You have to stay committed and encouraged during the process. Every promise requires a process.

James 1:3(AMP) - Be assured that the testing of your faith [through experience] produces endurance [leading to spiritual maturity and inner peace]. And let endurance have its perfect result and do a thorough work, so that you may be perfect and completely developed [in your faith], lacking in nothing.

THE MOMENT OF TEST AND TRIALS

In this relationship, you also will have to endure tests and trials that will test your love and dependency in our heavenly Father. Circumstances will arise that will test or check your "yes" or commitment to God and the call on your life. Sometimes this walk requires that you carry out tasks you won't always feel like doing. You will occasionally struggle with doing the right thing or being that mature or better person when someone does you wrong. You will not always feel like correcting and responding in love. You will not always feel like waiting for God. You will not always feel like serving in ministry. You will sometimes wish you could just have a "regular life." You will sometimes want to satisfy yourself or others before God.

All these feelings may arise, but they should not dictate your decision or actions. When you said yes to God, you made a predestined decision, that for God I live and for God, I die. You decided that no matter what, your trust and hope will remain in God. These tests will even reveal if your yes was out of convenience.

This will reveal your love for God and if you genuinely want him or just his hand. A relationship with God allows you to not only hope and want things from him but to know that his presence is more than enough. Loving and appreciating God because of who he is.

God wants to see if you are here to stay. God wants to see if you are willing to wait and endure the process, the attacks, and adversity. God builds strong soldiers that can fight because they are following and trusting the voice of God. God has to be able to trust you, and that's why he trains you. You have to get to a place of spiritual maturity.

1 Corinthians 13:11(KJV) - When I was a child, I spake as a child, I understood as a child, I thought as a child: but when I became a man, I put away childish things.

When you own the title of son or daughter of the most high king, you must allow him to train you just as he instructs mothers and fathers to do for their children. Your biological parents can only do their best for you; wherever they fall short, God will do all the rest. When you become new in Christ, God instructs us to become "like" little children, because children are more willing to be taught, and won't act pridefully as if they know it all. They take correction in all humility and are more vulnerable to listen to instructions coming from someone who has more wisdom than them. God trains up his children, he gives instructions and provides resources for us to learn and grow, so that when we get old, become spiritually mature, or walking in our callings, we will not depart or forget the things we learned.

When you own the title of being a child of God, you can trust that everything as part of the process is for your good. When you desire to walk in this new life led by Christ, it requires new teaching. To be taught, you must learn, you learn from experience, studying, and failures. So just trust the process. Your obedience to God shows that you trust his leadership and guidance in your life. Trust God and fight and do all it takes for your relationship and connection to him. He paid it all for you, now live for him wholeheartedly. Chase God and be a child after his heart and his will for your life. When you commit to God, your will and plans for your life cannot co-exist with his plan. There will be moments where you feel like something is good for you, but that doesn't always mean its God. Allow God to rewrite your story, let God be in control of your destiny, and depend on Him to lead you.

Matthew 18:3(NIV) - And he said: "Truly I tell you, unless you change and become like little children, you will never enter the kingdom of heaven. Proverbs 22:6(NKJV) - Train up a child in the way he should go: and when he is old, he will not depart from it.

EMPOWERED FOR A PURPOSE

To empower means to give the authority or power to do something. To make someone stronger and more confident, especially in controlling their life and claiming their rights. God empowers you to go after everything that is yours. He energizes you and equips you for whatever you want to do on earth. God gives you the power to speak life into dead situations. He empowers you to make and see something out of nothing. God gives us the power in our tongue.

You have the power to speak life over your life. You have the power to speak truth to any lie that haunts you. You have the power to speak peace over worry. You have the power to speak joy over sorrow. You have the power to speak strength over weakness. What are you doing with the power God gave you? If you speak death, worry, and complaint about a situation so that it will be. God gives you power, strength, and wisdom to do all the things he has called you to do. God has given you purpose and will guide you so that it can be fulfilled not only will he guide you, but he will supply all your needs.

Proverbs 18:21(NIV) - The tongue has the power of life and death, and those who love it will eat its fruit. Romans 4:17(KJV) - (As it is written, I have made thee a father of many nations,) before him whom he believed, even God, who quickeneth the dead, and calleth those things which be not as though they were. Philippians 4:19(KJV) - But my God shall supply all your need according to his riches in glory by Christ Jesus.

God will take you places that will leave you wondering how you got there. You will be able to say that it is only by the grace of God. Allow God to get the glory out of your life. When you live for God and in freedom, allow your behavior to reflect your freedom. When you are free in God, you get to choose what you allow in your life. You are empowered to achieve your goals and dreams in life. God empowers you to use your gifts in excellence. When you become confident, you can then walk your call out and believe that you are fearfully and wonderfully made. You can believe that no one can do what you do better than you.

With God, you become unstoppable. Somethings God calls us to do; we may not be able to do alone, or in our own strength, or by natural talent. So, God can use us even with our weaknesses and turn them into strengths. Sometimes it can be uncomfortable because we are used to only being good at our strengths. I believe God pushes and challenges us in our weakness so that we know it's only by His power that we can do it. Sometimes God calls us to do things that to the world we aren't even qualified to do. But God can use anybody and give them wisdom, and the tools needed to do it successfully.

1 Corinthians 1:27(NLT) - Instead, God chose things the world considers foolish to shame those who think they are wise. And he chose things that are powerless to shame those who are powerful.

1 Corinthians 2:9(AMP) - but just as it is written [in Scripture], "Things which the eye has not seen and the ear has not heard, And which have not entered the heart of man, All that God has prepared for those who love Him [who hold Him in affectionate reverence, who obey Him, and who gratefully recognize the benefits that He has bestowed]."

A relationship with God works both ways; it's designed to be reciprocal. Just like in a relationship on earth, building a relationship with God takes time.

In the relationship, you will get to know God more intimately. Learn God's character and strive to be just like him. You will learn his ways and learn to discern his voice. You will learn to trust him. You will learn how to lose your grip on trying to control your life and find security and a sure feeling of peace in God.

The first thing to understand is that God accepts you, just the way you are. God is a spirit, and he wants to work with the authentic you. Yes, you, with all your scars, problems, and hurt. Yes, you the one that feels overlooked, counted out, or isolated. He can use you! He has plans for you, your gifts, and abilities. God won't count you out, and he won't mishandle you. When you give your life to God, you are in good hands. If you are a person that might have trusted people in your past and they let you down, took advantage of you with their power, or hurt you, these may cause you to have trust issues. This is why at first, it can be hard to say you fully give your life to God because throughout life, you have tried to give people access to you, and later, you see that they didn't deserve it because of how they treated you.

To trust God, you have to stop comparing him to man. He will satisfy all your needs; he has the answers to all your prayers. He will guide you to an abundant life of prosperity. God's love for us is unconditional. He already knows our thoughts before we think them. He already knows that we are going to make mistakes and poor choices, yet he factored all of that in and still calls us his sons and daughters.

In relationships, we tend to look for the benefits and evaluate what is expected from each person. The benefits of God are endless, and his provision and favor over our lives grant us things that money can't buy.

All God's children are living to hear a well done at the end and to live eternally. In our relationship with God, he just wants us to serve him willingly. He wants us to be committed no matter what, and this is the same expectation we ask of God. When we mess up, when a crisis comes, when things are good and bad, we always look for the positive feeling of hope that God is with us and is working things out in our favor.

Therefore, for us to see how consistent God is with us, we must remain consistent with him. You must put in time, effort, and love into this relationship to get something out. You must make room for God, just like you desire him to make ways, bless, and open doors for you. Everything that God gives us, he deserves it in return. He deserves our lives, our time, our finances, and our gifts to be used for him.

In everything you do acknowledge God, consult him, ask for his guidance and advice. You have to be willing to listen and take his wise counsel. Do not try to do things without God and his principles because you will always be unhappy with the results.

Just trust that God's plan is better than yours, and any other external opinion. When your obedience begins to manifest things in your life, you will begin to trust him and his voice more. To know God's will for your life, you must build a relationship with him so that you can recognize his voice and respond. Then you will be able to test and prove his perfect will for your life.

Matthew 6:33(NIV) – But seek first his kingdom and his righteousness, and all these things will be given to you as well.

All that you desire in life will be given unto you when you follow Christ. There may be times where you feel like you lose or sacrifice so much, but it will be restored in another season. God's timing is perfect, and he has an appointed time for everything in your life.

Our God is a God of results. You will be able to enjoy the great things he has for you. A relationship with God is essential in your spiritual journey. A solid and firm foundation in God allows your heart to be close to him. God is looking for believers who seek to know him and want to serve him. God is looking for vessels that want to be used for his glory. God wants living sacrifices and bold children of His who will strive to fulfill a purpose.

Some believers speak good of God, but their hearts are far from him, God wants your heart. You must build a consistent relationship with God so that he knows where your heart is. Wherever your heart is, that's what you will be willing to make time for and serve.

So, when you feel like God is distant, or you can't hear him check the position of your heart. Also, check what or who you have speaking in your ear. Examine what you are focused on, and what distracts you. Always remember that if you do drift away, fall short, or put things before God, you are never too far to the extent that you can't turn back and get in alignment. No mistake or sin is too big that God won't forgive you; he already paid the price for that.

When growing in a relationship with God, remain patient, and don't get discouraged by comparing yourself to others. Every individual relationship with God is personal. You don't have to try to pray to God like someone else for God to hear you. God uses people in different ways. Therefore, give God what you have because that's all he expects. He doesn't want you to be anyone else. God calls us by name, not by groups. He knows, calls, and will judge everyone separately, so be yourself, and you will prosper.

Developing my relationship with God was important because, for so long, I depended on people who knew God or who were in leadership to go to God for me. That's because I was never taught to spend time with him for myself. I depended, looked to people to tell me their opinion of how I should live, and waited desperately for prophets to tell me God's will and instructions for my life. I consulted people for advice and methods on how I should live, pray, and handle situations in my life.

I grew up in church, lacking the proper way I should handle real-life situations. I was only taught what not to do and what to stay away from but never provided with the answer to how. My mind was so focused on trying not to mess up or disappoint so much that I felt like I was living on the edge as I was only trying not to make a mistake as if committing error automatically qualifies me as a horrible person.

However, that's how it feels when you are living trying not to err instead of learning how to go through life and overcome and be restored from mistakes and shortcomings. I was never taught what to do if you've had sex before marriage. Instead, I was judged. I was never taught how to deal with depression properly. Instead, I was just told to pray about it as if it were something that could easily be pushed away. I was never taught how to deal with being molested. It was something that was swept under the rug – something I was just supposed to get over.

I was never taught how to overcome temptation and impure thoughts; it was something that was not discussed as if we were too holy that the devil would never try to tempt us. I was never taught how to live for God, and still be in the world, but just not of the world. I only knew what I was taught, everything else I needed answers to, I got them from the world because the church did not provide it or didn't want to talk about it. When a church lacks transparency and is not able to put the word in perspective so we can relate it to real-life situations faced on a daily, we will never understand. After growing a relationship with God and learning his word,

I realized that his word is a manual to how he wants us to live our lives. I went to people for answers that only God, the one who created us all, could provide. You can have mentors and friends in life to help and inspire you, but you must develop your own connection to the source. You don't just wait till Sunday to plug into the source, you have to carry him with you throughout the whole week. This isn't just a relationship that you can treat as a one-night stand or friends only on Sunday.

I began to desire to know God for myself because that's when he became real to me. To believe and trust in something, you have to experience it for yourself. I heard testimonies about what God could do, I was taught about him, but I never truly knew him until I embraced a relationship with him.

You must go to the author and finisher of your life. Sometimes in life, we can find ourselves so anxious about what we should do next, and we feel like God wants to keep it hidden or a mystery to us. However, I believe when you get to know God, you will be able to see how persistently he speaks and will guide you. There are parts of your life that you are supposed to know, the only reason why you don't know is that you have not been spending time with the one who knows and made you. When you understand God more and his ways, you will have fewer moments of uncertainty and confusion.

Romans 15:4(AMP) - For whatever was written in earlier times was written for our instruction, so that through endurance and the encouragement of the Scriptures we might have hope and overflow with confidence in His promises. Now may the God who gives endurance and who supplies encouragement grant that you be of the same mind with one another according to Christ Jesus.

Chapter Six:

MAKING GOD THE FOUNDATION

Once you develop a consistent and robust relationship with God, you will be able to have successful and prosperous relationships, friendships, and partnerships on earth. When you learn to love God, you can love and treat others correctly. Your relationship with God and your faith should always be the foundation.

When pursuing relationships on earth, you will no longer have to fight to be loved; you will aim to love. Also, you will be able to trust that God will give you who you deserve to be loved by when you are ready to receive them. This is why singleness is so essential. There are things you must learn and deal with in singleness that shouldn't be brought into relationships or marriage. God will also show you when to let go of some people and environments. When you are becoming someone new, you will have to grow in new environments, which means some people and some habits you will have to leave behind.

Growth is not comfortable, but it works for your good. You have to realize that your obedience to God may disappoint and inconvenience some people. But when you are chasing after God, His kingdom, and its righteousness, those who remain were always for you, and those who leave may have been there only for a season.

1 John 2:19(NIV) – They went out from us, but they did not belong to us. For if they had belonged to us, they would have remained with us; but their going showed that none of them belonged to us.

When embracing this relationship with God, not everyone will support it; some may not understand. Be careful of those who try to dissuade you from doing the very thing that's best for you. This means that they rather see you stay in the state you are in instead of pursuing God to become a better version of yourself. Not everyone was expected to go with you on your journey of becoming who God called you to be. Not everyone is ready to go with you as they may still want to remain comfortable.

I struggled with this truth because I wanted those I loved to be excited for me and my growth in Christ. I not only wanted their support, but I desired to be able to relate to them. I wanted them to come with me and see my point of view, but I realized that our minds were no longer the same because carnal minds can't understand spiritual things. This was something I couldn't let discourage me. It was something that required prayer.

> *1 Corinthians 2:14(NIV) – The person without the Spirit does not accept the things that come from the Spirit of God but considers them foolishness and cannot understand them because they are discerned only through the Spirit.*

You have to understand that the same God that allowed you to see the truth is the same God that could do it for them. When I started going after Christ and serving God and pursuing a relationship by reading the word more while praying and serving in ministry at my church, some would have seen it as me overdoing it, but I learned to understand that it was only because they were not doing enough. I learned not to judge them or hold any grudge to the offense or the lack of support, but to continue to pray that they would grow spiritually and be able to experience God fully.

I had to learn how to cut soul ties with old friends, friends with benefits, and even family members and learn to love them from a distance. God's word instructs us to guard our hearts, meaning don't allow everyone access to it. Guarding your heart is important because everything you do comes from there. God wants our hearts to remain pure. Don't let the fear of someone's opinion of you to stop you or hinder you from pursuing your love for Christ.

Proverbs 4:23(NASB) - Watch over your heart with all diligence, For from it flow the springs of life.

However, God will give you ordained friendships and a community that will be able to go with you and hold you accountable every step of the way.

Sometimes, we may push away those who God placed in our life because they challenge us and are not the type of people who will agree with everything you do. Sometimes we may push people away because our pride or "trust issues" will make us believe that we don't need anyone. However, you do need people on this journey because two is always better than one.

Ecclesiastes 4:9-12(NIV) - Two are better than one because they have a good return for their labor: If either of them falls, one can help the other up. But pity anyone who falls and has no one to help them up. Also, if two lies down together, they will keep warm. But how can one keep warm alone? Though one may be overpowered, two can defend themselves. A cord of three strands is not quickly broken. Genesis 2:18(NIV) - The LORD God said, "It is not good for the man to be alone. I will make a helper suitable for him"

You just have to make sure that these are people that God ordained to be there. You don't need friends that will always tell you what you want to hear, but those that will be able to pray for you in time of need. You need those around you who see the best in you and can speak to the person you are becoming and not where you are now. You need friends that will be loyal to you when you are up and when you are down. You need friends that will support your vision and push you to become a better version of yourself. You need friends who will encourage you. You need friends that will be able to rejoice for you and not envy you. You need a friend that you can confide in, with no fear of being exposed.

A friend sent by God will push you towards him and never away from him. A friend sent by God will not be perfect, and disagreements may arise, weapons may form, but don't allow them to prosper. What's ordained by God will always remain, his plan will always prevail even over pettiness. I myself almost made the mistake of denying someone that God placed in my life.

In my freshman year of college, I met my roommate, who is now my lifelong best friend. However, in the beginning, I was not intentional about building a friendship because she challenged me, and when I mistreated her, or we got in an argument, the old me wanted to hold a grudge. She responded in love and waited for me to open up and talk about the issues. I used to be a person that hated confrontation, and I would do anything to avoid it. I was someone that was not good at communicating my problems. I was used to " letting things go and moving on."

On the contrary, she saw the good in me, even when I was at my worst. I had also pre-judged her because I saw that she was spiritual and loved God. However, because I was holding on to the church hurt, it changed my view on every Christian I came in contact with. This is because I used to see Christians as hypocrites and judgmental, but when I met her, she loved me with the love of God.

When I observed that our response to certain disagreements was different, I began to see that sometimes I could be the problem. I had to deal with some things in my heart so that I could receive the friend that God had placed in my life. She did not force God on to me. Her life pushed me to want to know him more. This experience taught me that sometimes we could mislabel people as our enemies, or see people as working against us because they challenge us. That was something I was not used to. God gave me friends that I needed. Had he left the picking up to me, I would've gone after people based on preference and not substance.

When you are a toxic person or operating out of hurt, you tend to attract and pick those you can relate to, but sometimes those people you choose are there to agree with and tolerate you operating out of hurt. People that complain and have pity parties need company. God sent me friends that I could grow spiritually and naturally and go through life with.

Everything God does is for a reason and a purpose. Even when disagreements arise, you should resolve it amicably because the good always outweighs the bad. Confront the issues in your life and heal, so that you can receive and enjoy the great things that God has for you. If you are hurt, prideful, or broken, it can affect your vision.

Many people desire the promises of God, but don't want to endure the process it takes to get there. Many people want to experience the abundant life God has promised them, but they do not realize that they must become free to receive these things. Some would rather stay in a place and mentality of hurt because it is comfortable and something they are used too. Walking in freedom becomes your new normal because when you give your life to Christ, he transforms your life. Being a child of God becomes your lifestyle. Your behavior becomes a reflection of your freedom.

God sent me to a church where I could grow and be cultivated. He blessed me with a leader that not only teaches the Bible but leads by example. God had to heal me, and then he was able to lead me to the place just for me. A place where I could be fed and taught the word of God. A place where I was not only a member, but I belonged.

From my personal experience, when I was asking God to put me in a place where I could grow, I began to battle with the Spirit of fear. I was afraid to go alone; I was overly concerned about what people would think of my decision.

However, at that moment, I had to do it afraid because I had to do what was best for me. When I followed where God was leading me, he confirmed that it was the place for me. I had to let go of perception, and remember that my goal was to please God, not man.

Another thing God taught me was that just because you are a part of a different church does not mean you have to be against another. God's word already talks about how there will be different churches, but we should all worship one God and in one Spirit.

1 Corinthians 12:5(NIV) - There are different kinds of service, but we serve the same Lord. Galatians 1:10(NIV) - Am I now trying to win the approval of human beings, or of God? Or am I trying to please people? If I were still trying to please people, I would not be a servant of Christ.

Every church is not for everybody, but I am a living witness that God will place you exactly where he wants you. No church is perfect because it is filled with imperfect people. When problems or disagreements arise, do not let the enemy trick you out of your spot. You have to learn how to forgive, agree to disagree, and respond in love. Having a great church home teaches you how to let go of pride and the spirit of offense so that you can take correction.

When you are surrounded by love and no judgment, you'll be able to be yourself and be fed both spiritually and naturally on your walk with God. Many do not want to go to church for many reasons. Some include the excuse that you could have church at home and that you don't need a church to have a connection with God.

However, the goal isn't only to have a connection with God; it's also to grow in God. Just like any relationship on earth, you don't just settle for connection, but you want to be joined together with someone you can grow with.

God wants us to fellowship and be led. He has designed the church and put pastors and leaders in place for a reason. How can you be led without a leader? How can you grow without nurturing? God wants us to be unified and be able to touch and agree and fellowship together. You cannot be groomed alone at home; you need spiritual guidance and a consistent covering. If you feel as though you lack friends, an inner circle, community, or a church that can go with you on your journey, don't be discouraged, just ask God to give them to you.

John 14:14(NIV) – You may ask me for anything in my name, and I will do it.

The community that God gives is supposed to love and not judge you, hold you accountable, support you, and push you. This community should also be actively pursuing Christ as well because two can't walk together except they agree. My relationship with God allowed me to become better in every relationship I had; a friend, daughter, sister and student. Having God in your life will allow all other things to prosper.

Part Three:

CONVENIENCE
TO
CONSISTENCY

Chapter Seven

THE FULL ARMOR OF GOD

There came a point in my walk with Christ, where I was in a relationship with him, but I began to realize that I often let my emotions and thoughts consume me, and I based my choices and actions on them instead of the promises that were over my life. When circumstances tested my faith, things did not happen as I planned, or I felt God was taking too long for something to come to the pass. I began to make decisions on my own, despite being vulnerable and not being at my best spiritually.

When we lose our focus on God and his will for our life, we might fall, and make some choices that would put our anointing at risk. That is why I am grateful to God for his mercy and his patience with me when I was in a phase where I did not see things as I should. God often uses certain situations and seasons of our lives to detox us, reset us, or bring us out of a circumstance that blinded us.

I realized that when I first answered God's call, I was desperate, and I humbled myself before his throne because I needed him and wanted him. So, I was willing to do whatever it would take to get what I needed from God. When I began to experience God for myself, and he began to work in me and answer my prayers, I realized I called and sought him only when I needed him, and that was usually when things were not going right in life. I would only talk to God, mostly when bad or unexpected things occurred. I would call on God for a "feeling" that would make me feel better. I realized that I only called on God, served him, or gave him all my attention when I needed or wanted something from him. I had a convenient relationship with God. However, in order to walk in God's will for my life, I had to become consistent. For us to get the full benefits of our relationship with Christ, we have to be all in. We need to become consistent with feeding ourselves daily with God's word, spend time with him in worship and prayer, and make fasting, devotion, and communion become something we do willingly and not as a ritual.

I became consistent with God and stopped seeking him just for his hand, but also for his presence and thanking him for just being a good God. As I progressed in my walk with God, I began to thirst for more experience of him all day, especially beyond the walls of the church. I wanted to see him work miracles and blessings in my academics, finances, career, talents, family, and my life as a whole. I knew that being a child of God meant I was no longer in a position to suffer and just barely get by in life because God promised a life of prosperity, which implies no lack. I desired to become an unmovable and unshakable tree so that when life challenges are thrown at me, I would stand firm and not let my emotions get the best of me. I had to make God my firm foundation and allow him to be the anchor of my soul. When I pursue consistency with God, my faith in him is cultivated.

1 Corinthians 15:58(NIV) - Therefore, my dear brothers and sisters, stand firm. Let nothing move you. Always give yourselves fully to the work of the Lord, because you know that your labor in the Lord is not in vain.

In order to track the growth of something, you must become consistent. This is the only way you can see and appreciate the results. The more you put in, the more you will get out. You must become consistent in your servitude to God. You have to strive to maintain a posture of gratitude and service and give beyond yourself. Becoming consistent with God allowed me to see that it is possible to live a life that is pleasing to him, without having to hide who I truly am. You also don't have to "have it all together" to be used by God. Bruised heels can still crush a serpent's head. That is, your pain or your weakness doesn't disqualify you or handicap you from being able to crush Satan and still walk into your victorious destiny. You have the power to put all that used to hold you bound under your feet and allow the enemy to lose over and over again because God has placed you in a winning position.

You must learn how to put on the full armor of God (Ephesians 6:10-18), to fight and tread over the schemes and strategies of the enemy. With God, your fight becomes spiritual. You are no longer fighting against physical people or things, but against spiritual forces of wickedness in heavenly and supernatural places. We are no longer fighting in the flesh, so we must be equipped in the spirit. When we are attacked in our mind, in our body, or life, our response must be spiritual. Your armor must be complete. You must have all parts to resist and stand your ground against the enemy because he will try to stop you. The enemy doesn't want you to win and believe it or not, the enemy knows what you are capable of when you have God. This is why he tries to keep you from the things of God.

It is crucial to have all parts of your armor because they all work together to produce results. After all, you are only as strong as your weakest part. Just like any armor, uniform, or outfit you put together, each part of it, is essential, and it has a unique purpose. Imagine if a firefighter went to put out a fire and had everything he needed but his shoes, chances are his feet will be burnt despite having every other thing. This implies, we could be so good at praying to God, but if we don't have the faith to believe, then we can't receive that which we pray for. If we are not allowing his word to get into our hearts, we have nothing to stand on. We have to show up to the fight with instruments or tools that are effective. For our weapons to be effective, we have to practice and train with them so we know how and when to use them. Sometimes we can focus on and highlight only our strengths and hide our weaknesses.

We must understand that God wants us to be whole, so we shouldn't be nonchalant, unaware, and ignore our weaknesses but work and rely on God to strengthening us in those areas. You must have the truth in your mind and have the integrity to do the right thing even when no one is watching. You need an upright and pure heart, and you also need to believe the good news of the gospel to challenge the enemy when he comes with his lies and deception. You need to have faith, and the helmet of salvation, so that you would never walk in shame or guilt because Jesus already paid the price for your sins. The word of God is a tool you cannot do without either. It instructs us to pray with perseverance and a sober mind, in every season and not just for ourselves, but also for all God's people.

God wants us to be aware of both our strengths and weaknesses and strive to be well-rounded in him, willing to be used in any capacity he calls us to. For instance, in the past, I had found myself saying to God, "You can use me, have your way," but when he asked me to pray for someone else, I would back out because I didn't see praying for someone else as a strength I possess.

However, that you are not comfortable, strong, or confident in an area doesn't mean you can't be used in that area. You have to be willing to allow God to use you when you are uncomfortable. How else would you expect to grow in such an area of weakness? When God shows you your weaknesses, your response should be to ask God to strengthen you, and you work on it, not hide it.

God teaches us how to fight, and he shows us how much power we have. For so long, we can battle with the thoughts that we aren't good enough, that our love life will never succeed, and that things will never work out for us. You are and can become what you think. This is why the enemy attacks our mind because he knows that when he has our mind, he has dominion over us and can control us. When we have to make choices, we need to make sure we consult God so he can guide us, because sometimes, the choices we make based on our prefer- ences are often not what we really needed.

God gave us the power to challenge our thoughts and call it under subjection and make it obedient to Christ, or the truth. When a thought comes in your mind, you must evaluate by asking yourself, "Is this true? Is this something that will bring me pain? Will I regret this de- cision?" After you evaluate, challenge or reaffirm it with the truth. Don't allow the enemy more time than he al- ready had to play with your mind, by allowing thoughts to make you worry and anxious. Don't be afraid to call

out or expose the enemy; don't give him that much
power over your mind and your destiny.

> *2 Corinthians 10:5(NIV) - We demolish arguments
> and every pretension that sets itself up against the
> knowledge of God, and we take captive every thought
> to make it obedient to Christ.*

Chapter Eight:

REMAIN HUMBLE, SURRENDER YOUR GIFT

When you become consistent with God, always remember to remain humble. Humility is the state of modesty, without an excess of pride. Don't allow the gains and elevation of this world take you away or make you forget God. We have to stop forgetting to thank God after we have received what we asked him for. When we ask and receive, we shouldn't stop serving him. One thing I had to learn was to stop putting my gifts, passions, talents, and desire to succeed before God because I need God to operate effectively in, to handle, and achieve them. Dancing is something I have been naturally good at, and so I was making sure I did everything to perfect that gift.

I was committed to going to practice and rehearsals and literally found myself running around campus to make it to step practice, play practice, choir rehearsal, and every other activity related to dancing. When I injured my foot and was instructed to wear the most uncomfortable walking boot I ever experienced, it was the moment I realized that God allowed it to happen so that I could slow down, sit down, and rest in his presence. When I was told by the doctors that it would take 6-10 weeks to heal, all I could do was cry because I had so many planned performances I would be missing out on. I was confused, but instead of worrying about where or who the attack was coming from, I began to focus on what I could do at that time because, after all, the circumstance was out of my control. I was frustrated and sad because I couldn't understand how God could take me away from my gift. It was my life. In that vulnerable time, the enemy tried to torment me with the thought that I had done something to upset God and that he no longer loved me or wanted to use me. The devil tried to make me feel like I no longer had a purpose. I later realized that the circumstance was only temporary, and that God allowed it to happen to get my attention because I was not spending enough time with him. He got my attention right there in my resting place. When I was taken from what I wanted to do, what I worked so hard for, I realized that I had to order my priorities and make sure always to keep God first.

God doesn't just want your gift. He equally wants you to have a good character and strong foundation in him while operating in it. My foot accident was definitely a test of my faith and my commitment to God. Once I realized what I was supposed to learn through it, God blessed me with quick healing. Much quicker than the doctors predicted. I became a walking miracle because what ordinarily would take 6-10 weeks to heal only took 4 weeks.

As believers, we have to understand that whatever God allows would never be intended to harm us, it is for a purpose, and it is always for our good. As you learn lessons in your walk with Christ, make sure you apply the knowledge after the test, or you will always end up having to re-take the test again. After I came out of the boot, naturally, I had to learn and practice how to walk again and strengthen my foot, which was being restricted from being used at its normal capacity. So spiritually, I had to apply the new knowledge in my walk, always to keep God first. Allow God to be a part of your career goals, business plans, and whatever you are passionate about because doors will open, and favor will follow you when God is in it.

At that time, when I was unhappy with the situation and I couldn't operate in the gift that I was "most comfortable" in, I couldn't let my discomfort take away my praise that God still deserved. Just because God allowed situations to occur, doesn't mean it will end in disaster. It may feel like a setback, disappointment, or failure now, but it is a necessary preparation to catapult you into your purpose. If you still have breath in your body and promises over your life, you still have a purpose, and God is not done with you. Keep the faith and keep going; this is not the time to give up and go backward. Anytime a circumstance comes that you don't like, dedicate time to trying to ask God what he is trying to tell you or what he intends for you to focus on in that season.

God doesn't want to harm you, but he uses circumstances to get our attention. When situations arise, don't look, and ponder on the negative. Look for the good or the lesson in your discomfort. God gives you a gift so that he can work through you and get the glory, not so that you can take him out of the plan. Surrender your gifts, plans, and ideas to God. When you keep God in it, there is a guarantee that it will prosper.

CONSISTENTLY TRUSTING GOD'S PLAN

When I became consistent in my walk with God, I also had to become consistent with trusting him. Sometimes, we can limit the places of our life in which we trust God while we take matters into our own hands in other areas. The more you grow and mature in God, you begin to see that you can no longer be in control. Living for God is a continuous and daily choice. Following God means you move from being a babe in Christ to a disciple by putting his word into practice and being obedient to his instructions.

Luke 9:23(NIV) - Then Jesus said to his disciples, Whoever wants to be my disciple must deny themselves and take up their cross and follow me.

Following God means you choose his way of doing things over yours. For instance, you are no longer in control of how you treat or respond to people, you must respond with the mind of God, even when you don't want to. Your response in love will always be more powerful than responding out of spite, hate, or offense. God doesn't even want you to offer your gift while you are still holding grudges against his people. God teaches us to forgive totally, not forgive and still hold a grudge against those who offend us or even treat us wrong. God may even lead you to pray for those that once hurt you. It's all about the posture of your heart; you have to grow a heart for his people, which requires selflessness.

Forgiveness doesn't mean you give the person access to hurt you again, but you must release the feelings of resentment you have against them. It takes so much more energy and effort to hate someone than to just forgive and love in spite of it all. Sometimes, our pride won't allow us to forgive because we feel we didn't deserve the mistreatment, but we ought to remember that God forgives us every time we do wrong or make a mistake. We must imitate the posture of God's heart in our lives. When problems arise, God instructs us to reconcile, which means to restore or to cause to coexist in harmony. His word tells us that he will only forgive us as we forgive those that trespassed against us. Because we are forgiven by God, we must learn to forgive people.

Matthew 5:23(NIV) - Therefore, if you are offering your gift at the altar and there remember that your brother or sister has something against you, leave your gift there in front of the altar. First, go and be reconciled to them; then come and offer your gift. Matthew 6:12(NIV) - And forgive us our debts, as we also have forgiven our debtors. Some people like chaos and drama and thrive in these environments.

Some people find unforgiveness comfortable and normal because the world makes it seem as if you should hold a grudge to prove a point so that they will never hurt you again. We have been made to think that forgiveness and responding in love makes us weak. When really, it shows how strong we are. If you don't learn how to forgive in this world full of unperfected people, your relationships will always be hindered from thriving because you don't understand the power and the principle of reconciliation. We so easily choose to stay mad at people and think that blocking or "cutting them off" will solve the problem. You can try to physically move away from or leave such a person out of your life, however they would still mentally, and emotionally, have power over you. Holding on to that pain as an excuse not to forgive ends up hurting you more.

We sometimes get so used to operating in the chaos that when we have peace, we get uncomfortable because it feels abnormal. We have conformed to the patterns of the world and have gotten so used to hating one another and living with no peace because we are still blaming and holding on to hurts and the offenses that were caused. This is why many families are divided and dysfunctional because no one is dealing with the matters of their heart. God tells us to seek peace and pursue it, which implies we ought to follow or go after peace. God urges us to walk and live in peace. Peace is not the absence of problems, it is the presence of God in the midst of those problems.

Psalms 34:14(NIV) - Turn from evil and do good; seek peace and pursue it.

You can no longer be in control; in God, you must lose yourself, to find yourself in him. When you begin to delight yourself in God and the things of God, your desires will begin to align with his plans for your life. You will no longer have to wonder hard about what God wants or has for you because when you begin to see and think like him, making the right choice will become natural. Be obedient to the instructions for God's plan for your life.

Proverbs 19:21(NIV) - Many are the plans in a man's heart, but it is the Lord's purpose that prevails.

You have to understand that you are no longer operating and sticking to your desired timing; you now have to trust God's timing and not be in a rush. Rushing things will lead to disappointment, which would lead to you waiting longer than necessary. While you wait, you must keep the faith and serve God and his people. Sometimes, we can become anxious about something that was promised because we can't see it yet, but do not worry, only trust God. Humble yourself and believe that God will raise you up in "due time" if you don't quit.

You may get discouraged when you feel you are waiting for things to happen for you; that's why God instructs us to give our cares to him; he already knows how we feel. God is not offended by your questions when you genuinely express your feelings to him. Your feelings are valid. You don't have to hide them. You shouldn't just let them control the choices and decisions you make. You shouldn't let your emotions lead you. You have to allow God to lead you and bring your emotions and flesh under his submission. Peace comes when you give it all to God, knowing you are where God wants you to be. Being in alignment with God is the specific place where he can bless you. To stand firm in your faith, you must live according to your beliefs, and speak it until you see its manifestation.

1 Peter 5: 6-7 (NIV) - Humble yourselves, therefore, under God's mighty hand, that he may lift you up in due time. Cast all your anxiety on him because he cares for you
Philippians 4:6(NIV) - Do not be anxious about anything, but in every situation, by prayer and

petition, with thanksgiving, present your requests to God.

Fully trust in God with all your heart when you are faced with troubles. He has a plan and purpose for you. You would just have to go through specific processes to get there. Before our salvation, when we were in the world, we were in control of our lives, and we had a sense of independence. However, giving our life to God means we have to let God be the Lord of our life. Allow God to be the potter, and you the clay.

On the potter's wheel, you have to go through some things, some molding, and some shaping before you get the finished product, which is a masterpiece. In your going through, allow God to continue to work on you. He has overcome the world, and he is in control. When God is birthing or producing something through us, it may not always feel good, but when the process is over, we would be better for it. We would no longer feel overwhelmed by the pain we felt during the process because we would now relish in the joy of the finished product. So, we have to keep pushing.

John 16:21(ESV) – When a woman is giving birth, she has sorrow because her hour has come, but when she has delivered the baby, she no longer remembers the anguish, for the joy that a human being has been born into the world.

John 16:33(NIV) - I have told you these things so that in me you may have peace. In this world, you will have trouble. But take heart! I have overcome the world.

Chapter Nine:

GOD DOESN'T NEED A MICROMANAGER

Trust that God is leading you in the right direction. Look at how far he has already brought you. You won't miss a sign from him because it will continue to get bigger. One thing I have realized is that though I would say I trust God; I still try to meddle with his affairs in an attempt to help. God doesn't need us to micromanage him concerning our life. A micromanager is someone who tries to control every part of a project by getting themselves involved and in close supervision.

He is someone who feels their help is always needed, even if it is just a little. A micromanager is someone that keeps checking anxiously, not realizing that God is already in the process. He or she is someone who doesn't fully trust that the person in charge can actually get the job done.

In the Bible, God promised Abram and Sarai a child, even though Sarai was barren, and Abram was old. Abram and Sarai looked at the circumstances and began to take matters into their own hands to "help" God fulfill His promise, instead of trusting in the word God gave them. Sarai believed that her barrenness meant God restrained her from bearing a child. So, she gave her maid to her husband so that He could conceive through her. Often when we try to help God instead of trusting him, our plan or suggestion of help might make sense to us at the moment. But, if God gave you a promise, who are you to think that he would birth it through someone else other than you. Here Abram and Sarai's faith were being tested in a situation where circumstances seemed like it was against them, but they learned that if God said it, he would work it out. God didn't need their help to fulfill his own promise. He needed them to be still and know that he is God.

Genesis 16:2-5(KJV) - And Sarai said unto Abram, Behold now, the Lord hath restrained me from bearing: I pray thee, go in unto my maid; it may be that I may obtain children by her. And Abram hearkened to the voice of Sarai. And Sarai Abram's wife took Hagar her maid the Egyptian after Abram had dwelt ten years in the land of Canaan and gave her to her husband Abram to be his wife. And he went in unto Hagar, and she conceived: and when she saw that she had conceived, her mistress was despised in her eyes. And Sarai said unto Abram, My wrong be upon thee: I have given my maid into thy bosom; and when she saw that she had conceived, I was despised in her eyes: the Lord judge between me and thee.

For God to work it out, you have to take your hands off it. After you take your hands off it, you must be fully obedient so that you can get the full expected result. In Numbers, chapter 20, when Moses and Aaron were leading those into the promised land when they faced opposition, backlash, and complaints about the way they were leading, they always went back to the source for clarity, direction, advice, help, and reassurance. This is proof that we shouldn't allow critics to discourage us from doing what God told us. Here you have to realize that when you are on assignment from God, you must be able to hear his voice because when others rise against you with their opinion, you can stand firm and know that you have to do it God's way. This is why it is so important to grow a relationship with God, so you can recognize and discern when he is talking. If you are unsure of who is talking to you, you can easily be influenced by others, and that can take you out of alignment with God. So, make sure you are always connected to the source.

God gave Moses simple instructions, "Speak to the rock, and it will pour out the water." Instead, Moses "took the staff, raised his arm, and struck the rock twice with his staff," and water did gush out. Here, Moses took what God gave him to do and did the extreme when God only required little. Moses used what was more comfortable, instead of using the power in his tongue. The expected result was produced because God already gave his word. However, Moses and Aaron suffered a consequence for their disobedience. Moses lost the benefit to see the promised land, and Aaron died.

Numbers 20:12(NIV) - But the Lord said to Moses and Aaron, "Because you did not trust in me enough to honor me as holy in the sight of the Israelites, you will not bring this community into the land I give them.

When on assignment from God, you must be sensitive to his voice and instructions. God wants you to operate out of power, not performance. Sometimes, we overthink or over-do what God requires us to do, due to doubt or lack of trust. We feel we have to do extra. We even disregard instructions and try to act based on memory or the way we are used to handling things, instead of acting on what God has told us. When you are sensitive to God's voice, he can trust that he can get the unexpected things done through you because you will listen to him no matter what. We may also try to please people, or we may be used to doing things our way and still getting results but just not as we should.

Developing consistency with God is all about having faith and allowing it to be cultivated. When we begin to trust God, and he instructs us on what he wants us to do, we begin to make excuses claiming what we have is not enough to carry out what he has called us to do. But what we minimize, God can maximize. What we see as little, God can do much with. So, start what God has instructed you to start. You do not need to know all the details of how it will work out, trust that you have all you need to know for now, and you can step out in faith and obedience. Don't despise or look down on small beginnings; everyone and everything had to start somewhere. Just understand that if you start something, it has the potential to grow, if you don't start it all, it would just be wasted potential. So, don't allow fear to hold you back.

IT'S NOT JUST ABOUT ME

When you become consistent, you will begin to experience God's provision and favor in your life. When we become consistent, we will also realize that this walk with God, and our purpose aren't just about us, but it is bigger than us. God wants us to serve others. You can serve wherever God places you; in church, through ministry, at your workplace, in your business, and to those who are new in the faith. Avail yourself to be used by God in any capacity, even if it makes you feel uncomfortable. One place I began to see God work through me was on my job. This was a job I didn't like that much, and I used to complain about it. We have to learn how to stop complaining about the very thing God gave us. Even though the job I was at wasn't my "dream" job, the less I complained, the more I began to see why God had me there. I was someone that could speak life into people's situations and pray for those who needed it. Allow God to use you right where you are, I can promise you, it is preparation for where you are going.

As God teaches you and allows you to serve others, don't forget to take care of yourself. When serving and in a ministry, you have to remember to continue to stay filled up, and ask God for overflow, or a fresh anointing, because you cannot give out of anything, you will burn out. It is like having a car, and you fill it up with gas. When your gas tank begins to approach "E," you know that for your car to continue to run, you must go get more gas. Don't allow yourself to run empty; ask God to keep filling you up again.

There was a man in the Bible named Elijah, who was obedient and devoted to God. While on his journey, he got to a point where he became tired and felt like he had enough and wanted to quit. God provided and strengthened Elijah to endure in his weak moment. God instructed him to "Get up and eat" because, for him to finish the journey, he needed more substance within him. Likewise, we must be honest with ourselves and understand that living for God and doing his work takes diligence. You must continue to feed and take care of yourself both naturally and spiritually.

> *1 Kings 19:4-5(NIV) - while he himself went a day's journey into the wilderness. He came to a broom bush, sat down under it, and prayed that he might die. "I have had enough, Lord," he said. "Take my life; I am no better than my ancestors." Then he lay down under the bush and fell asleep.*
> *1 Kings 19: 7(NIV) - The angel of the Lord came back a second time and touched him and said, "Get up and eat, for the journey is too much for you."*

While becoming consistent with God, we have to make sure that we don't begin to become comfortable. Seasons will change, and God may shift some things in our "daily routine." God may call and require you to do different things in different seasons, and it may not always match other people's instructions and expectations. God may call us to pray more times a day or call us to abstain from certain things. He may call us to spend more time than usual in his word. God may call you to serve in more than one ministry or take on a leadership position that comes with more responsibility. God may call you to rebrand or redevelop your business, he may call you to take a break from dating, or he may tell you to start a blog. Understand that everything God calls you to do is for a purpose and he will equip you for it. If you want more of or from God in your life, it will cost you something, which could be time or your desires in that season. You have to choose to move and do what God says or live life comfortably unfulfilled because you did not fulfill your purpose.

Chapter Ten:

LOSING FOCUS

Growing in God, some situations may arise that would make us lose focus. I tend to lose focus when I begin to put what I want and my desires before God's desires, instead of waiting on his appointed time. I begin to lose focus when I put other things before God. I began to become impatient and lust after things that were not for me. But impatience usually births disobedience, and our disobedience can blur our vision. Then you will begin to convince yourself that you are still in alignment with God. My disobedience to his instructions caused me to mishandle what he gave me. When we lose focus, we can begin to conform to the patterns of the world or operate in our flesh.

Sometimes, when things in life don't go as planned, we have to ask God to renew our mind about a situation. Renew means to reaffirm, re-establish, restore for freshness, revive, and resume after interruption. We need to ask God to help us resume with the truth that has been interrupted by lies. When you renew your mind and realign with God, you will be able to receive his will or his instructions on what you should do. Other times, we may feel like we have lost sight of our purpose, and we began to seek God on what we should do. We need to remember that God says after our mind is renewed, we would be able to test and approve his perfect will for us. So if you try something that you thought was in his will and it doesn't prosper, or you are still confused and uncertain, that might not be his plan for you because whatever God tells you to do, when you obey, he will confirm and approve it. That is our way of being able to understand how God can work in our lives when we began to see the results and the manifestation of our obedience.

Naturally, I struggled with staying focused when trying to get an assignment done for school. I had to get in a quiet place and eliminate all distractions to get it done efficiently. I realized that when there are distractions, I get hindered from producing at my best. God doesn't want us to multi-task on our own terms because, as soon as you lose focus on God, things will begin to fall apart. Allow God to multi-task, and you just stay focused. God intends us to stay focused on him even when we feel like we are under pressure. The pressure should continually push you to pursue the promise, not walk away from God. He also wants us to stay focused even when things that "look" like trouble arises. In Matthew 14, the familiar story of Peter teaches us never to lose focus on what we know, distracted by what we see with our natural eye. Peter saw Jesus walking on water, and asked him, "Lord, if that is you tell me to come," Jesus responded, "Come" and Peter stepped out in faith and began to walk on water. Here, Peter was the only man other than Jesus, known to ever walk on water. Sometimes, you have to be willing to take the risk even when no one else has done it before. Peter had faith, but he lost focus. Peter saw the wind, and he let it take his eyes off Jesus, who was allowing him to walk on water. When Peter took his eyes off the source, that was when he began to drown. Don't give attention to distractions because they will be the cause of your fall. Often, what we see has the power to scare us or discourage us to the point that we begin to sink in something that God was just allowing us to do so effortlessly. Peter didn't sink because the power of the wind or the "distraction" overtook him; he began to sink because he doubted God.

Matthew 14:31(NIV) - Immediately Jesus reached out his hand and caught him. "You of little faith," he said, "why did you doubt?

DON'T CHASE A TITLE, CHASE GOD

Following God's plan for our life requires patience and perseverance, just like anything else we may want in life. When serving God and being involved in a church or ministry, sometimes being in the forefront as a minister, pastor, preacher, evangelist, or deacon seems like something we all want because of the benefits that we see come from it. We sometimes believe holding these titles is the only way God can use us. God doesn't just need people in the church to lead. He needs us to go out into all the world to share his good news. We need to be a minister wherever we are. Some want a title to make them feel secure or confident in their walk with Christ. Some want a title so that they can have fame and fortune for their own glory. Permit me to tell you this, "Don't wait to be acknowledged, to prepare for the call. Don't wait for a title to make you." A title only enhances who you are. You must become and operate in who God wants you to be before the title. The title or the acknowledgment should only confirm who you are.

Many may want the title and the harvest, but they don't want to be processed and have not learned to discipline their flesh. We are called to be set apart. We can't be like everybody else. As you began to mature in Christ, a servitude lifestyle should already be practiced. You should focus on becoming faithful in doing the things of God when no one is looking or forcing you to do them. Holding a title isn't as easy as perceived; it is not for the feeble-minded or self-ambitious. It takes work, patience, processing, test, trust, discipline, risk, and sacrifice. Some wait for a title or try to operate in a call and help/lead others, and yet they have not even been processed. Having the title is not just about you; you are only the vessel being used. God can use anybody to get what he wants to be done on earth, so be grateful that he chose you.

Instead of waiting on the call or elevation, work with what is in your hands. Do all you can with what God has already given you. God knows if he can trust you to take care and cherish the little, then he knows he will be able to trust you with more. When you do things, do them to glorify God, not to be seen or glorified by people. The title doesn't just come with the benefits you perceive; it comes with responsibilities. Just understand that the elevation you want has prerequisites.

You have to master your now before you can move to your next. Learn in your now to prepare for your next. Whatever you are learning now has to be carried and executed in your next. God is a God of level up so he will prepare you for your next. Do not be so caught up and anxious about what you want and see in your next and miss what's in your now. Cherish and embrace every season you encounter because they are all important. You can't skip steps with God. Instead of chasing a title or position, chase God, learn how to be a child of God first. The title doesn't make you; you make the title. You need to have substance. Some are looking for a platform and a microphone, the microphone will only produce or enhance what is in you, when you have a title with responsibilities you have to continue to pursue Christ and be obedient in good and bad times. Even when you want to give up, you have to be built not to crack easily under pressure. Everything that we set as big goals in life requires prior steps to get there.

You can't learn how to be in a successful marriage without learning how to be successfully single first. You can't just buy a house without first learning how to save and budget money. You can't just get a license without first learning how to drive. You cannot get your dream job without having the prerequisites just as you can't graduate from college, without going through each semester. You can't get to your next until you get through your now. When navigating through your now, don't be lazy or delay obedience because you will just delay your promise. Sometimes, we allow ourselves to think we have all the time in the world to get things done, but when God says move, we must learn to answer without hesitation.

God might show you the end of a journey but not the process or show and take you through the process and not tell you the end. God doesn't usually tell us the whole plan, that's why sometimes we may not understand, but God knows all, and he is intentional about what he is doing. Sometimes, God doesn't really show me the end because if he did, I would probably self-sabotage the promise or no longer look to him for guidance for how I am going to get there. So, I have learned to consult God before doing anything. Do what God told you to do, and allow Him to call you, and catch you being obedient and humble. It's in the moments where we stop worrying, that things start happening for us. In the Bible, David was one of the sons of Jesse, the Bethlehemite, that God instructed Samuel to anoint the next king over Israel. Out of all the sons that were observed or assumed to be chosen because of their outward appearance, David was chosen because of his heart. Guess what David was doing while Samuel was looking for him to be anointed for his next? He was tending to his father's sheep. Being obedient and diligent at what God had given him to do. Samuel sent for David because they couldn't proceed without him. To others, David didn't seem to be the one that would be chosen, but God's purpose always prevails.

> *1 Samuel 16:10-12(NIV) - Jesse had seven of his sons pass before Samuel, but Samuel said to him, "The Lord has not chosen these." So, he asked Jesse, "Are these all the sons you have? "There is still the youngest," Jesse answered. "He is tending the sheep." Samuel said, "Send for him; we will not sit down until he arrives." So, he sent for him and had him brought in. He was glowing with health and had a fine appearance and handsome features. Then the Lord said, "Rise and anoint him; this is the one."*

Understand that when God is ready to elevate you, you won't miss the call if you are in alignment. No one else will be able to take your spot when God anoints you to do it. Even when those around you forget you, not refer you, or think you are unqualified, none of that would matter because God does, he will send for you, and nothing will be able to proceed until you step in the room. When you are anointed for the call, position, or assignment, understand that God will equip you with all you need, what you have is enough. In the next chapter, after David's anointing by Prophet Samuel as directed by God, David was chosen by God to fight a Philistine. Some doubted David's ability to fight and win because of David's age, job, and stature compared to that of a huge warrior. He didn't doubt himself because he had already experienced God rescue him and allow him to overcome other situations. Here, David had to apply prior experiences that God brought him through to allow him to have the courage and the faith that the same God who did it before can do it again.

Trust your process of going through and never forget where God has brought you from because it will increase your faith, and you will need it in the future. David could trust in God because he had experienced his work. As David was preparing to fight, Saul tried to give him armor that he thought he would need. However, David was not used to fighting a battle with human-made armor. He knew that because he had God, he was going to use the weapons that God trained him with. So, he prepared for battle with five stones and a slingshot.

Use what you know, not what others think you will need. Write the vision that you have, not what others suggest you should do. Apply for school or that job with what you have and stop waiting for what you think you need. When you begin to recognize that you are not fighting alone, but that you have God on your side, you can trust that whatever giant comes your way would be defeated because God is bigger and more powerful.

1 Samuel 17:38-40(NIV) - Then Saul dressed David in his own tunic. He put a coat of armor on him and a bronze helmet on his head. David fastened on his sword over the tunic and tried walking around because he was not used to them. "I cannot go in these," he said to Saul, "because I am not used to them." So, he took them off. Then he took his staff in his hand, chose five smooth stones from the stream, put them in the pouch of his shepherd's bag and, with his sling in his hand, approached the Philistine. 1 Samuel 17:45(NIV) - David said to the Philistine, "You come against me with sword and spear and javelin, but I come against you in the name of the Lord Almighty, the God of the armies of Israel, whom you have defied.

Do you trust and believe in God's power? Sometimes, the odds might come up against you, what's in front of you may seem big and impossible, but with God, all things are possible. Naturally, it may be impossible, but the God we serve operates in the supernatural.

Matthew 19:26(NKJV) - Jesus looked at them and said, "With man, this is impossible, but with God, all things are possible.

Chapter Eleven

HINDERANCES
WHILE PURSUING

A nother thing we must become consistent with is our tithe and offering to God. A tithe is a re-quirement. If we don't tithe, we are robbing God, and our finances can be cursed because of disobedience. If you don't tithe, you are blocking your own blessing. Tithing is for your protection because when you give God what he requires, your finances can be blessed. Tithes and offerings were one thing I used to struggle with because I was not always a cheerful giver. I was okay with spending my money on the things I wanted and needed, but when it came to God, the posture of my heart in giving was wrong. I dealt with the spirit of greed, and I realized that we could sometimes make money our god. Money meant a lot to me because I didn't grow up with an overflow of wealth. When I finally started earning something for myself, I became stingy because I valued it too much and feared losing it. I had to learn to stop putting my trust in money and began to put my trust in God to provide for me.

God can take you places and do things in your life that money can't buy. An offering is a gift brought to God beyond our tithe. Sometimes when I gave offerings, sometimes I would give in doubt with no expectation for God to bless me. Sometimes, I would give in fear because I felt like what I had was not a lot. I had to stop giving grudgingly and give cheerfully and with expectation. Once I understood the principle and the power of giving, I was able to give with a good attitude. I realized that if my hand to give was always closed. Then it could never be open to receive either. God will give seed to the sower. I realized the power of giving and started seeing God really allow harvest to produce in my finances. I started seeing God's unmerited favor in my life. I began to desire God to use me like a river, something that he could get the resources of money through and not for me just to keep alone.

Sometimes in life, God will then instruct you to give or sow into others beyond yourself. You must be very sensitive to God's voice because he will instruct you on where and who to sow into. You want to make sure you sowed into fertile ground that will produce something in your life because you were obedient and willing to sacrifice. The gain you receive will not always be financial; sometimes, it could be having more peace, or God could perfect those needs you are so concerned about.

Malachi 3:8-12(KJV) - Will a man rob God? Yet ye have robbed me. But ye say Wherein have we robbed thee? In tithes and offerings. Ye are cursed with a curse: for ye have robbed me, even this whole nation. Bring ye all the tithes into the storehouse, that there may be meat in mine house, and prove me now herewith, saith the Lord of hosts, if I will not open you the windows of heaven, and pour you out a blessing, that there shall not be room enough to receive it. And I will rebuke the devourer for your sakes, and he shall not destroy the fruits of your ground; neither shall your vine cast her fruit before the time in the field, saith the Lord of hosts.
Luke 6:38(AMP) - Give, and it will be given to you. They will pour into your lap a good measure— pressed down, shaken together, and running over [with no space left for more]. For with the standard of measurement you use [when you do good to others], it will be measured to you in return.

Now, I will discuss somethings that I have battled with when trying to go after God's will for my life and walking in my purpose. One thing that I am still working on is to stop striving for perfection to qualify me for my call. I had to stop excepting circumstances to be perfect, to determine if I was going to proceed and endure. When you are a perfectionist, and things don't go your way, you can begin to talk yourself out of the things God has for you. When you hold yourself to an unrealistic standard of perfection, and you mess up, you will spend so much time beating yourself down, while God is fighting for you to get up.

At times, when we experience God so much, we can feel entitled, feeling things will just be handed to us easily. However, that is a misconception, you have to put work in to get to your promise, and you have to get used to doing things even when you are uncomfortable and unready. Sometimes when God promises us things, we have a perfect plan in our head of how we want it to go. There is a process to the promise; you have to get through that to receive what God has. Sometimes, our goal to be perfect or trying to meet a standard of others could hinder us from pursuing our gift because, in our head, we believe we aren't good enough. Whose standard are you holding yourself to? God or man?

Growing up dancing since the age of 13, I used to dance everyday practicing and to rehearse all my steps until they were perfect. I took all genres of dance and at one point, I even used to travel around with different teams for competitions. When I went to college, I was not training as much as I used to, and in a way, I begin to doubt that I could still operate in this gift because, to me, my technique wasn't as good as others. That was where God allowed me to see that I didn't just have a gift to dance, but he also gave me the creativity to choreograph and teach others.

I realized that the more God used me in this gift, the more I recognized that I was not just an average dancer, but I was someone who was able to minister through dance. I realized that when I danced, chains began to break, lives were touched and changed, and sprits were moved. God allowed me to see that I could be used through my gift. My goal had changed from striving just to be a perfect technical dancer, but also to pursue my relationship with Christ because I was no longer dancing just to perform or because I was good at it. I was dancing from a place of understanding and power. I saw God use my gift in a totally new way, instead of desiring just to be known and have followers, I wanted to be impactful. I wanted to be able to lead and change lives with God. So instead of striving to be perfect, strive to progress and grow in the Lord.

Another thing that can stop or hinder us from walking in purpose is the effect of comparing ourselves to others. I was someone who would talk myself out of doing things because I saw "everyone else was doing it already." I used to get discouraged because I thought that someone else was more effective and that there was no need for me to bother. I realized that comparing myself to other people slowly began to kill the purpose inside me. I had to understand that just because someone else was doing it didn't mean that I couldn't. I had to remind myself that God calls us by name, and no one can do what you do like you do. I had to remember that I was always striving to be a better version of myself and that I should allow myself to be my own competition.

I had to understand that God puts everyone on this earth for a purpose and that everyone's purpose isn't going to be achieved in the same way. Everyone's purpose and assignment are different, many people can write a book, but I had to understand that my book can reach those that maybe others can't. I had to learn to own my purpose and walk in my lane confidently no matter who else was doing it. This walk is selfless, but you must still stay focused on what God anointed you to do. So, stop using "well, everyone else is doing that" as an excuse. God doesn't want you to try to be like anybody else; the only way you are able to prosper is if you continue to be yourself and go after and fulfill purpose.

Allowing other people's success to hinder me was also a place where God showed me that I was still dealing with insecurities. Meaning, I wasn't always secure in who God called me to be. I grew up always feeling that I was not good enough, and always trying to find validation from people. Once I began to know God, I understood that I was loved and worthy. Even though insecurities can try to creep back into our lives when God is pushing us to do something bigger than we could ever imagine, we must stay in agreement with who God says we are. So now, every time an insecure thought comes into my mind, I have to continue to reaffirm to myself who I am in Christ.

Another thing that can hinder you from pursuing purpose is the fear of not having support. We sometimes think we need support as a form of validation that we are doing the right thing. God telling you and giving you the desire to do it should give you all the support you think you need to go ahead. I struggled with this for a while because I really wanted to see people happy for me. I was so focused on waiting for those around me to believe in the new me, that I was losing faith in myself. Instead of fearing that no one will support you, just do it and watch God work. He will allow people that you don't even know to support you. God will send those who will support and push your business or idea.

Besides, another hindrance can be laziness. Laziness says I can do it, but I chose not to because I don't "feel" like it. Being obedient to God won't always feel convenient. Pursuing purpose won't always feel good. I've realized that the moments I pushed through against my emotions were the moments the greatest things were produced.

The people you are connected to can hinder you. Un-ordained business partners can hinder you because if you aren't on one accord, it will never work. Conflict will always arise. Even the people and things we are holding on to sometimes could be the very thing that is hindering us from producing what we are asking God for. Ask God to help you reevaluate your network of people, and who you are letting speak over your life. Ask God for discernment and so that he can lead you in making connections. I came to a point in my life where I began to ask God to remove every weight that is slowing me down on my race. When he began to remove things I liked and enjoyed, I realized that sometimes I couldn't see what was slowing me down because I enjoyed it so much. The more I began to delight in God and his will, my desires began to change. I stopped waiting for people to validate me, and I came into an agreement with who God says I am.

> *Philippians 2:13(NIV) - for it is God who works in you to will and to act to fulfill his good purpose.*

God says we should ask whatever we wish, but some of us don't like asking in fear of receiving a no. We must understand that God's no and yes are both for our good. His no and wait are to protect us from things we can't see, his yes allows him to get the glory. When you remain in God, and his word abides in you, what you ask for will begin to line up with his will for your life. Be ready for him to blow your mind because he can do so much more than what we ask for.

> *Ephesians 3:20(NIV) - Now to him who is able to do immeasurably more than all we ask or imagine, according to his power that is at work within us, to him be glory in the church and in Christ Jesus throughout all generations, forever and ever! Amen.*

One thing that I have learned to appreciate God for more was directing my steps even when it wasn't what I naturally wanted. There have been times in my life where I had to sacrifice relationships or to go forward with my plans to do what God told me to do first. At first, I saw it as a punishment that I was doing something wrong, but the more I began to seek God, the more I began to understand that everything he leads us to do is for a reason. So sometimes, God will take somethings away, or allow things to be on pause for us to focus on him.

Now, every time I experience things not going the way I envisioned, I begin to raise my expectations because I know this is a set up for God to really blow my mind. So, even if it hurts or you get disappointed, it is more beneficial to obey what God is telling you even though what you were doing felt so good and right. The more I began to obey God, the more I began to trust his instructions because I saw what it began to produce in my life.

Chapter Twelve:

NEVER LOSE YOUR ZEAL

As you remain in God, never lose your zeal for him. When you feel like giving up in your walk or even on your assignment, remember why and how you started and just continue to strive in purpose toward your promise. Continue to grow in knowledge and understanding. Allow his word and instructions to be a lamp unto your feet, so that your path will always remain bright.

Psalms 119:105(KJV) - Thy word is a lamp unto my feet and a light unto my path
Romans 12:11(NIV) - Never be lacking in zeal, but keep your spiritual fervor, serving the Lord.
Philippians 1:9-11(NIV) - And this is my prayer: that your love may abound more and more in knowledge and depth of insight, so that you may be able to discern what is best and may be pure and blameless for the day of Christ, filled with the fruit of righteousness that comes through Jesus Christ—to the glory and praise of God.

As I became more consistent with Christ, somedays, I began to face the ongoing daily challenge to remain steadfast in my growth in him. To be steadfast means to be devoted, dedicated, and faithful. Sometimes, I wondered if it would be better just to be a "regular person" I realized that being regular would just make me go backward. I remember that when I was regular and didn't serve or know God in this capacity, I was broken, I had no peace or purpose. We have to remain devoted and faithful to reach the promise and to allow salvation to have its full effect in our lives. Salvation was given so that we can be free and remaining consistent with God keeps us free.

When you began to grow and glow in Christ, don't forget that it is also your responsibility to share the good news with others. You are qualified to be a minister of salvation through Christ. Don't just keep it all to yourself; be willing to share, help, and pray for someone else. When you begin to serve God, you can then realize that what God wants to do through you is so much bigger than you. Even if you can't physically share his good news by word of mouth, allow your life to attract people to Christ. Your life should be an example of the living word of God. You are no longer living to satisfy yourself, but you are living for Christ, and your standards come from the Holy Bible.

Before you can actually talk, preach, or try to teach someone about Jesus, your life may be the only thing they see. Allow your life to be the light everywhere you go. Allow your light to shine so bright that the whole world knows who you are living for. One thing I have learned when trying to help or bring people into Christ is that I have to be careful that I am not trying to be God for them. Our duty is to share the news and plant the seed and allow God to do the transformation. If you always find yourself trying to "fix" people or trying to explain yourself to people concerning the word of God, that may be a sign to move and allow God to finish the work that he started in them. You have to give others time and room to grow in Christ as well. You have to learn how to become patient. You also should understand that you are not meant to be everybody's hero because then they will never be able to learn and apply knowledge. After all, you keep trying to save them. If they never suffer the consequences, you will always find yourself rescuing them.

Proverbs 19:19(NIV) – A hot-tempered person must pay the penalty; rescue them, and you will have to do it again.
Proverbs 20:30(GNT) – Sometimes it takes a painful experience to make us change our ways.

Often times, we can become a hindrance or a crutch to their relationship with Christ because we can become their "god." In all you do, always encourage, and empower people to get to know God for themselves. Your responsibility is to motivate them, hold them accountable, share your wisdom, and be there as a support. I have found myself caring so much for people that I wanted more for them than they wanted for themselves. In such moments, you must seek God and ask, "Is this person slowing me down, or is this an assignment from you?" Because on this walk with Christ, we can be so concerned about helping people, but sometimes we are just wasting our breath because some people just like the "idea" of change and how great it looks but are unwilling to pay the price and do the work it takes.

These people you are giving so much to sometimes, are really only draining you out. If you are having a hard time trying to hold people accountable. Ask God to give you the wisdom to handle such a situation. Don't allow shame, guilt, or fear of being judged hinder you from being able to be transparent with people about your testimony of where God has brought you from and your challenges on your walk with Christ. When you are trying to help people or lead people in Christ, you first have to be an example for them to see what God has done in your life.

> *2 Corinthians 3:6(AMP) - He has qualified us [making us sufficient] as ministers of a new covenant [of salvation through Christ], not of the letter [of a written code] but of the Spirit; for the letter [of the Law] kills [by revealing sin and demanding obedience], but the Spirit gives life.*
> *1 Peter 3:15(NIV) - But in your hearts revere Christ as Lord. Always be prepared to give an answer to everyone who asks you to give the reason for the hope that you have. But do this with gentleness and respect.*
> *Matthew 5:14-16(KJV) - Ye are the light of the world. A city that is set on a hill cannot be hidden. Neither do men light a candle, and put it under a bushel, but on a candlestick; and it giveth light unto all that are in the house. Let your light so shine before men, that they may see your good works, and glorify your Father which is in heaven.*

We must realize that God wants the world to be saved; he doesn't want to see anyone perish, so he gives us time to get it right. When you remain in God, you begin to think like him and have his desires. God desires for his good news to be shared, and he can do it through you, you have to be willing and patient.

2 Peter 3:9(NLT) - The Lord isn't really being slow about his promise, as some people think. No, he is being patient for your sake. He does not want anyone to be destroyed but wants everyone to repent.
Mark 16:15(NIV) - He said to them, "Go into all the world and preach the gospel to all creation.

Chapter Thirteen:

CONSISTENCY: PERFECTION VS. PROGRESSION

Being consistent with God does not mean you will be perfect. You will make mistakes; you may fall. But with Christ, you can get up again! When you didn't have God, it was easy for the enemy to keep you bound in your shame, but because you have God, you can repent and be forgiven. We are forgiven. Jesus already paid the price. God remembers our sins no more, so don't stay down rehearsing your mistakes, get up, and learn. When we fall, our job as followers of Christ is to acknowledge and take ownership of our wrongs and repent. God responds to repentance by forgiving us. He doesn't hold our wrongdoings against us. God knows our hearts. He knows the difference between us being sorry just because we got caught and being sorry because we actually want to change and get it right the next time.

The beatitudes say that blessed are those who mourn for they will be comforted. When we sin, it produces a burden that we can carry for so long. With God's forgiveness, that burden can be lifted. Let's take a look at the prodigal son, who was once a lost son who wasted and mishandled his inheritance. Once he returned home, his father forgave him and embraced him on his return. There was also a woman caught in the very act of adultery, and God never condemned her for her sin, he forgave her and gave her instructions to sin no more. Also, there was the case of the thief on the cross who was forgiven right before his death because he acknowledged his wrongdoing and asked God to remember him, and Jesus responded that he should be with him in paradise.

The truth is, Jesus came to the world for sinners, like you and I. He didn't come to justify the sin, but he came to free us from it and transform us. Nothing can separate you from God's love for you. Sometimes, we watch what God can do for others, but we still don't feel we are worthy of God turning our mess into a message. However, I can testify and say that I once was lost and now I am found. God used and still blessed me despite all my flaws and shortcomings. I am a living testimony that the same grace is available to you. We have to stop allowing ourselves and others hold us to who we used to be and agree with how God remembers us. He said he remembers our sins no more, and that he can purify us from all unrighteousness.

Isaiah 43:25(NIV) - I, even I, am he who blots out your transgressions, for my own sake, and remembers your sins no more.
Colossians 2:14(KJV) - Blotting out the handwriting of ordinances that was against us, which was contrary to us, and took it out of the way, nailing it to his cross.
1 John 1:9(NIV) - If we confess our sins, he is faithful and just and will forgive us our sins and purify us from all unrighteousness.
Matthew 5:4(AMP) - Blessed [forgiven, refreshed by God's grace] are those who mourn [over their sins and repent], for they will be comforted [when the burden of sin is lifted].

When you aim to be consistent with God and his ways, you will be blessed and satisfied—being consistent means to be compatible or in agreement with something, unchanging in nature over time, acting, or done in the same way over time. The aim of being consistent isn't to be perfect. You are aiming to be consistent in serving God, aiming to be consistent in allowing your faith to grow. Aim to allow God to remain in all of your relationships. Remaining consistent in how God instructs us to live wherever we go—remaining consistent on seeking to be in right standing with God. God is the one who is sustaining you. Remain in agreement with who God says you are and in agreement with your commitment to Christ no matter what.

> *Matthew 5: 6(AMP) - Blessed [joyful, nourished by God's goodness] are those who hunger and thirst for righteousness [those who actively seek right standing with God], for they will be [completely] satisfied Proverbs 19:8(NIV) - The one who gets wisdom loves life; the one who cherishes understanding will soon prosper.*

As a follower of Christ, you must be in the attitude of Christ. God gives us the beatitudes in Matthew 5: 1-12, which is an outline of the attitude, a settled way of thinking or feeling about someone or something, we should have. These beatitudes are instructions and guidelines of how we should live. Just like when people say we are representations of our parents or organizations we are a part of, you are no longer your own, but you belong to God. When we are followers of the most high God, we must act accordingly. When you live how God destined you to be, you will be blessed.

Chapter Fourteen:

WHAT KIND OF FRUIT DOES YOUR LIFE PRODUCE?

WE ARE THE SALT OF THE EARTH

It's one thing to know you have a purpose in God. It is another to understand and get wisdom and instructions for fulfilling your purpose. The most crucial part is that you put consistent faith, action, and effort into pursuing your purpose. This means you can't give up. God calls his disciples the salt of the world. Salt fulfills its purpose of adding flavor to food. God places us here to add to the world by living and not just existing without purpose. I now understand that the moment we don't feel like we have a purpose, we feel like we are not good for anything, so why exist? Without God, you have no purpose and live an unfulfilled life. With God, you have a purpose, and it shall be fulfilled.

Matthew 5:13(AMP) - "You are the salt of the earth; but if the salt has lost its taste (purpose), how can it be made salty? It is no longer good for anything but to be thrown out and walked on by people [when the walkways are wet and slippery]."

To prosper in God, you must first become a planted tree willing to bear his fruit in your life. Only planted trees can produce fruit. Only well-kept and protected trees can produce good fruits. Many trees can produce fruit, but not all fruits are edible, that is, they are unsafe to eat. Your fruit or what you produce proves that you are a disciple. Your fruit will be remembered. Your fruit can exemplify, your actions, success in your career, the impact from your non-profit organization, how many lives and souls are changed and saved through your mentorship, or the fruits of the spirit.

Galatians 5: 22-23(NIV) - But the fruit of the Spirit is love, joy, peace, forbearance, kindness, goodness, faithfulness, gentleness, and self-control. Against such things there is no law.

The fruit represents whatever is produced through you. Knowing and walking in your purpose allows you to produce. What should keep you motivated is where you started. Remember, your tree once started as a seed planted in faith that broke through the soil. This plant began to grow and mature and develop and see the purpose; once you reach and get through the growth requirement, you can multiply and produce.

HOW IS THE FRUIT PRODUCED?

One crucial element in fruit development is the production of flowers. However, for fruit trees to produce flowers, it must have all its growth requirements met. The requirements are adequate light, water, proper soil conditions, nutrients, and a favorable temperature. Adequate means satisfactory or acceptable in quality or quantity. You need enough, which implies, lacking none. If you don't get what you need in this season that can produce stunted growth, which is impaired growth. Impaired growth is a product of poor nutrients and repeated infection, without such nutrients, plants have a difficult time absorbing water, producing healthy foliage, and developing strong roots. As a result, their growth is stunted. All these conditions are the things experienced when you are aiming to build a consistent relationship with God.

These conditions are also the process of getting to the flowering phase, and fruits develop from flowers. Once you get to the flowering stage, you are still not done. The flowering stage can be the moment you find and know your purpose. Fruit production can't happen until pollination occurs. Pollination is the fertilization, which is the process of fertilizing the egg or the flower—the fusion of gametes to initiate the development of a new individual organism. After pollination occurs, if conditions remain favorable, an embryo begins to grow, eventually progressing and developing into the mature fruit.

The production of your fruit is affected by what is planted around you, the production of fruit increases when another variety is planted, so surround yourself with fruitful trees. Meaning you can be surrounded by those who already have wealth, get around those who have been where you want to go. You can't let other people's success intimidate you; you can watch them win and be affected by their wisdom. Their presence is more effective when you are motivated but don't try to imitate, steal, or envy their fruit.

Other factors influence fruit formation, both negatively and positively. Pruning keeps the tree healthy overall by cutting away dead, weaker, or overgrown branches. When you remove the weak, you allow room for growth—pruning influences which direction the plant will grow. When you make a cut, you stop growth in one direction to encourage it to grow in another way. Shaping is the practice of training living trees and other plants into artistic shapes and useful structures. Pruning and shaping are needed because if a tree is left on its own, it is likely to develop many non-fruiting shoots and branches. Pruning and shaping may not feel good, but it is necessary to make sure we stay in alignment and progress in God. Pruning and shaping come from God.

Pest and disease control are also necessary to help ensure good fruit. Pests and insects will weaken and kill the tree and attack the fruit directly. This sounds like the enemy who works hard to kill your purpose, your vision, and the things that you produce. The enemy doesn't just attack your mind. He wants to attack, hinder, and slow you down from pursuing God's will. The form of control you need can represent your church, spiritual covering, and mentors that can cultivate you and the production of your fruit. The pest control can also represent the full and complete armor of God.

Temperature and nutrients also influence the production of fruits, so you must be aware of what season you are in so that you can take proper precautions. Unseasonable frosts can damage blossoms and reduce or even prevent fruit production. This is the time when you have to be a proactive grower and cover or guard yourself against these brief, but damaging moments. You have to be observant of the season you are in and what you can handle during it. You have to be protective of yourself when you are in a season where you are under pressure, when you are vulnerable, going through a season of purification, or having a weak moment.

In seasons of healing, you need to be protected or covered because if you don't get through true healing, it will get worse and mess up other things in the future. In seasons of development, you must be covered because God has to sharpen you and not put you in the forefront when you are not ready. In seasons of preparing for ministry, you have to be covered and focused on God. Different seasons and assignments require different instructions. If you don't get what you need in these seasons, you will not be able to be successful in your next. If you don't learn how to have a relationship with God first, no other relationships can prosper. If you don't allow God to be your foundation, apart from him, you can't do anything.

> *John 15:5-8(NKJV) - I am the vine; you are the branches. If you remain in me and I in you, you will bear much fruit; apart from me, you can do nothing. If you do not remain in me, you are like a branch that is thrown away and withers; such branches are picked up, thrown into the fire, and burned. If you remain in me and my words remain in you, ask whatever you wish, and it will be done for you. This is to my Father's glory, that you bear much fruit, showing yourselves to be my disciples.*

Your fruit is what determines who you are planted in. What kind of fruit comes from your tree? What are you producing? How will you be remembered? What will you do with what God gave you? Remain planted in God, follow his instructions, and you will bear much good fruit!

ACKNOWLEDGMENTS

First and foremost, I would like to acknowledge and give all glory and honor to God for allowing this book to be produced through me. I would like to also thank those he allowed to be in my corner to support and push me when I wanted to give up. To my sisters, Corrina, Eniah, and Amirah thank you for your encouragement and advice when I needed it most. To my parents, Erica and John, for helping me, providing advice, encouraging me to take breaks, and always believing in me. To my life-long friends, Lawrion, Lauren, Faith, Asha, Natonia, and Jillian thank you for your support, late-night phone calls, encouragement and most of all your prayers. To my Pastor and First Lady thank you for cultivating me and my faith to allow me to walk in my purpose and be all God has called me to be.

Made in the USA
Middletown, DE
30 September 2020